Readers are leaders. ☺

Best wishes,

- Linda
El Awar

Graduating from Google
Leadership Lessons
By Linda El Awar

To my Mom and Dad, for their never-ending love and support.

Table of Contents

PREFACE

When I first visited the Harvard Business School, I was surprised how often the students and staff referred to the school's Masters in Business Administration (MBA) program as a "transformational experience." I heard that phrase repeatedly throughout my time at Harvard, and it was in fact quite true. I was not the same person when I graduated. I had developed new ways of thinking, different perspectives to approaching problems, and a global viewpoint. I had bigger goals and dreams. I was fired up to work my way through corporate America!

However, as powerful as this transformation was, it was minor compared to the transformation I experienced during my time as a Google employee. I am often asked, "What was it like to work at Google?"

The truth is, I never really thought about what it was like to work at Google until I left the company. While I was there, I was too engrossed in my daily work to step back and think about how I was changing as a person and as a leader. Though I regularly thought about my business learnings, the fact is I had gained an entirely new education by working at Google, and it was not just in technology and digital media.

I had learned about working with people.

It was as if I had spent years in college earning another degree, and graduated with an emphasis in leadership. Working at Google was all about working with people. It sounds so simple, yet in fact it was quite complex. Every day was like attending class and every interaction was like a pop quiz. My people skills were regularly tested. And when it was time for me to move on, the feeling was bittersweet, just like graduating from Harvard. I had built relationships that I knew would last a lifetime. My heart was filled with happy memories. Part of me never wanted to let go.

It was nothing short of a privilege for me to work at Google, but it is an even greater honor for me now to reflect upon my experiences and share my learnings, which are lifelong leadership lessons.

TRY SOMETHING NEW

I went to the Harvard Business School (HBS) with the intention of becoming a marketing leader. I assumed I would end up in a traditional marketing role with a consumer packaged goods company. I never thought of joining a technology or media company, nor did I consider myself to be an early adopter of technology. But when I began searching for a summer internship while studying at HBS, I decided to open myself up to unexpected opportunities, and that is what allowed me to begin a fulfilling career.

HBS did not allow students to miss class in order to meet and interview with prospective employers. All classes were taught by the case study method, which meant that students' class participation was not only critical to their learning, but to that of their classmates as well. Nevertheless, the school understood the importance of helping its first-year MBA students secure summer internships. As a result, all classes were canceled for a full week early in the second semester, a time literally known as "Hell Week" amongst the students and faculty.

I was a first-year MBA student at HBS in 2006, and Hell Week that year was beginning on a Monday after the Super Bowl. First-year MBA students were divided into groups of 90 students who attended the same classes together every day, and each grouping was called a "section." My class section was holding a Super Bowl party Sunday evening in one of the dorm lounges, and I was looking forward to it. Like most HBS students, I had spent a significant amount of time preparing for Hell Week and had approached it as a full-time job search instead of "just a summer internship." But unlike most MBA students, I knew I did not want a career in consulting. I declined all offers to interview with consulting firms that winter; I did not even consider consulting as a backup option. Prior to attending the Harvard

1

Business School, I had worked for a major automaker for two years plus a summer internship during college. I had loved my internship, but the full-time position had been a nightmare for me, mostly due to the corporate culture. I had learned the hard way that culture was a key ingredient to my happiness on the job, and I did not think I could find what I was looking for in a consulting environment.

My goal was to secure a position within marketing, though what in particular I was not sure. I had quite a few interviews lined up, mostly with consumer packaged goods companies, all of which touted how fabulous their corporate culture was. The recruiters all seemed genuinely nice during the meet and greet sessions, and I could see myself getting along with these people. However, I was still nervous about the potential outcome...I did not want to be the only student at the end of the week without a job offer. Deep down I knew I was not especially thrilled about my upcoming interviews. I wanted something different, but did not know exactly what that was. Hence, I was looking forward to relaxing at the Super Bowl party before the madness began.

Unfortunately, the party was anything but relaxing. Those interested in marketing jobs took notes during all the commercials in case they came up during interview discussions. Those interested in consulting compared thoughts about the case interview process. I suddenly felt overwhelmed. I just wanted a couple of hours to relax with friends. Instead, I found myself submerged in an extremely intense study session. I managed to stick it out until halftime, and then made an excuse to sneak home early. Alas, Hell Week had begun, and it was already living up to its name.

Ironically, it was freezing cold during Hell Week that year. The majority of interviews were conducted on campus, but a few were held in nearby hotels. I had a couple of interviews on Monday and Tuesday, but did not feel excited about any of them. I had not clicked with any of the companies yet, and I knew if my heart was not into it, I could never perform to my full potential. Wednesday came, and in my business suit I tip-toed through the snow to a cab stand, off to an interview at the DoubleTree hotel with another consumer packaged goods company.

I had high hopes for this interview, as I had enjoyed meeting the employees at a previous company mixer. The position was in Chicago, a city that I loved and was close to my hometown in Michigan. Unfortunately, I felt no chemistry at all as I sat through the interview. I was waiting for an adrenaline rush to know I had found a firm with the right fit, but it never happened.

Beyond frustrated, I trudged through the snow back to my dorm room. Salt from the sidewalk on my suit was the least of my concerns. I was interviewing with some of the most well-known brands not only in the country, but throughout the world. Yet not one of them seemed appealing.

I made it back to my tiny dorm room, which was so small my father joked that it was a prison cell. I kicked off my boots, plopped down at my desk, turned on my laptop and called my family. My supportive parents were anxiously awaiting a full report on the day's interview. I wanted to be enthusiastic for them and tell them it went great. But I could not. As I relayed the events to my father, he tried to focus on the positive aspects and encourage me. I did not want to hear it and began zoning out. I started to scan through my email as he spoke and an odd message caught my eye. The sender's name was "Starla." No last name. The message was one line, reading, "are you interested in talking about opportunities at google?" That was it. No proper punctuation or grammar. I instantly thought it was spam and became angry. "I can't believe someone is trying to play a joke on me about jobs this week!" I exclaimed to my father on the phone. "I'm moving this to the trash!" And I did.

"Wait a minute," he said. "You don't have anything to lose." Gradually, he convinced me to move the message back to my

3

inbox, and eventually respond.

The next thing I knew, I had a call scheduled with the mysterious Starla. I had no idea who this person was or how she had found me. I still felt that I was part of some cruel hoax and was waiting for the bomb to drop.

Starla had presented the call to me as an informational chat. I was too naive at the time to understand that meant "phone screen" to see if it was worth the time of a Googler (a Google employee) outside of human resources to formally interview me. My naiveté worked to my advantage as I was not even the slightest bit nervous. I was able to relax, be myself and answer her questions with ease. Starla mentioned she had discovered me through one of the resume books published by HBS, and I recall the shock at realizing that someone actually read those resume books, followed by relief that I had taken my resume submission seriously.

I expected her to conclude the call by advising me how I could formally apply to the open internship position. On the contrary, my surprise continued as she stated I had cleared the first round and she wanted to schedule time for me to speak with a couple of Googlers. They were in California and I was in Boston, so a phone call was scheduled for 7pm Eastern/4pm Pacific on the following Monday.

HBS provided students with an opportunity to be matched up with career coaches. I had a fabulous one who was a volunteer alumnus and based in California. She was ecstatic when I gave her the latest update. However, I still was not sure how serious this opportunity was.

Monday rolled around, and classes had resumed. Many people had consulting and investment banking offers lined up. Many others were still interviewing. I tried to avoid discussing Hell Week as much as possible with my classmates. I do not enjoy boasting or whining. Luckily my neighbor and closest friend at HBS felt the same way. We kept each other sane with pep talks and our mutual love of sports.

I had worked ahead of the coursework as much as possible during the weekend to clear my evening for the Google interview. After class, I continued to prepare for the interview. I cleaned my dorm room spotless so I would not have any distractions during the call. I considered putting on a suit to ensure I was in the right mindset. In the end, my jeans were just too comfortable and I did not change.

The time had come and my phone began to ring. An Account Planner and Account Manager from Google were conducting this interview. But it felt much more like a candid conversation. I was again at ease and able to answer all of their questions confidently. They were serving automotive clients who were marketing across Google's various digital media properties, and they needed someone with automotive expertise to join the team. I was from Michigan, the heart of the auto industry, where we say gasoline runs through our veins. During my time at the automaker, I had gone well beyond the confines of my role and studied the industry diligently, including all aspects of the automotive value chain. I knew I had the automotive expertise these Googlers needed. However, I also knew that knowledge was not enough to join this team. Equally important to them was the cultural fit.

I sensed the cultural questions during our conversation, but I did not know if my answers were what they wanted to hear. Nor did I make an effort to tell them what I thought they wanted to hear. I spoke what I truly believed, as I think an interview is also an opportunity for a candidate to evaluate the prospective employer. It is not a one-way street. I figured if my answers did not match their expectations, then it was not the right place for me to be. I had never worried about cultural fit when I interviewed to join the automaker. I refused to make the same mistake twice.

The conversation seemed to fly by as I genuinely enjoyed speaking with the Googlers. I immediately emailed sincere thank you notes and waited to see what would come next. I assumed more interviews would be required if they liked me, but I did not assume that I had qualified for the next round.

I was wrong on both counts. I suddenly had a summer job offer from Google. I could not believe it. This seemed too easy, too good to be true.

I almost declined the offer.

I had been truly miserable during my time at the automaker. While I learned a great deal about the importance of leadership, I learned it from a lack thereof. It was an environment where peers tried to bring you down instead of collaborate, where managers gossiped about employees instead of leading by example, and where innovation was nonexistent and often frowned upon. I vowed when I came to HBS that I would not go back and would put as much distance between myself and the industry as possible. And yet suddenly I was being sucked back in. I did not want to forever be just an auto girl. It seemed like suicide.

I discussed my dilemma at length with my career coach and one of my favorite professors. My career coach was so excited about Google that I felt her advice was too biased. She said I should just try it and get Google on my resume. In her opinion, the worst case scenario was that I hated the job but got a chance to spend a summer in California. She did not convince me. It was my professor who resonated with my nervous thoughts. He advised that the job could be done with any type of client, not just auto. The skills were transferable. This was about breaking into the technology space, not getting stuck in automotive.

He sold me. I accepted the position. It all seemed surreal, but I was off to California. I booked a room at an ExtendedStay Suites and a cheap rental car for the summer. I was still skeptical, and wondered if I would even survive the summer. Little did I know this was the beginning of something extraordinary and transformational. In retrospect, I shudder to think about what I could have missed out on if I had not been bold. Do not be afraid to try something new. The cost of playing it safe all the time could far exceed the cost of daring to change.

MASTER THE BASICS

I knew that one of the key reasons Google had hired me for the summer was because of my extensive automotive knowledge, and I was ready to share that expertise. But I had no background in technology or digital media, and I fully believed I would not succeed at Google until I mastered the basics.

I managed to make it to the office early and without getting lost on my first day. I had arrived before the front reception opened and did not even have a Google badge yet to get through the secured doors. I caught a kind person in the hall who guided me to the office café. Google preferred to call them cafés as opposed to cafeterias, a tradition started by one of their first chefs in Mountain View, since the food and atmosphere were in fact far superior to that of a traditional cafeteria and focused on bringing people together. My team happened to be enjoying a bagel breakfast in the café when I walked in and introduced myself as the new intern.

I felt completely out of place. Everyone was dressed casually...flip flops, shorts, t-shirts...my boss was the most formally dressed in casual capris, sandals, and a t-shirt. Nevertheless, I felt a surge of excitement despite my awkward professional clothes. This was not your average corporation. The café was buzzing with positive energy and good vibes, which is quite rare in most offices on a Monday morning.

I sat down with my new boss, who outlined two ambitious projects for the summer. The projects were intended to benefit the national Google Automotive team, not just those based in California. My local team instantly took me into their fold, and I was humbled by their pride in having an MBA intern on their team. However, a hard lesson from my time at the automaker led me to make a concentrated effort to minimize any references to my future degree amongst colleagues and clients. When I first joined the automaker full-time, my boss sent a fax (remember those?) to all of the dealerships I would be working with to announce my arrival. He did not share the fax with me until after it had been sent. It detailed my educational background and honors and emphasized my superior business skills. Many of the dealers I would be working with had never gone to college; however, they had spent their entire lives immersed in the industry. Furthermore, the majority of my dealerships had been run by family members for multiple generations. The idea of a 22-year-old kid who had never spent a day working in a dealership serving as their business consultant baffled and offended them. They wanted nothing to do with me before they even met me. I spent months convincing them that I appreciated their work history and had a great deal to learn from them. Eventually they saw my sincerity and our partnership began, but that fax cost me months of extra work and lost sales that could have easily been avoided.

I had succeeded at the automaker despite my rough beginning because I completely engrossed myself in the industry. Every day I dedicated time to reading as much as I could about the automotive business, and when I first began almost all of my personal time was dedicated to becoming an "industry expert." I reached a point where I could question the automaker's Vice President about legislative matters impacting the automotive business yet still discuss return on investment with a service technician. This knowledge is what led my dealers to eventually accept me, and I knew I had to do the same thing at Google. I had little knowledge of the digital space, and I understood this was a mandatory basic step for me to succeed at Google.

Thus, I decided to tackle all of the AdWords certification courses. AdWords is Google's core Search revenue generating product, and most advertising agencies require their employees to complete this certification. My team served many advertising agencies, and many of the materials I was assigned to produce that summer would be presented to those agencies. How could I expect any of them to take my work seriously if they saw that I lacked their basic digital knowledge?

It was actually a bold risk to announce I wanted to spend my first week mastering AdWords. At the time, it was not a requirement for the interns or full-time employees, though years later that changed. In addition, studying for these online lessons had the potential to significantly delay my projects. Nevertheless, it was well-worth the risk. The certification process came up as a topic of discussion at my first client event. I immediately bonded with the agency staff as we shared our study strategies and I was able to answer their questions about AdWords. I had set the foundation for acceptance. To ensure that my Google peers also approved of my work, I put extra time into my projects on the weekends to meet all deadlines.

While it was a big risk on my part, it was also one of my first great Google leadership lessons. I took it upon myself to tell my boss that I was going to spend my first week learning AdWords. I took the time to master the basics. That is where I saw many younger employees fail later when I was a manager. They were so accustomed to being challenged in college that they wanted to demonstrate superior knowledge immediately. They did not want to take the time to learn the boring basics, which on the contrary made them appear arrogant and ignorant instead of brilliant. Take time in the short-term to create a basic knowledge foundation for yourself, and you will establish yourself for long-term success.

CHART YOUR OWN COURSE

Despite producing fantastic results during my internship, my career at Google almost ended before it even started. At the conclusion of the summer internship program, Human Resources made it clear that they were only hiring on an as-needed basis, and they could not anticipate the company's personnel needs between now and summer of 2007, when the intern class would have completed their MBAs. I wanted to work for Google, but I could not risk waiting until graduation to see if Google might have a job opening for me. I had to create my own opportunities and chart my own course.

Rather than accept Google's stance, I began communicating with a few other interns I had met who also wanted to return to the company. They were equally frustrated and together we made our opinions known. As a result, HR reconsidered and decided to create a new position specifically for us interns, but we had to apply and go through another round of interviews before we could officially become Googlers. There were no guarantees.

It was embarrassing to come back to the Harvard Business School at the end of August empty handed as almost all MBA interns receive a full-time offer letter at the end of the summer. If someone did not receive an offer, well, you can imagine the speculation of how poorly he or she performed. I found myself constantly justifying to fellow classmates how Google only hired on an as-needed basis. Another department within Google had been running a separate intern program for years, and a few Harvard MBAs had participated in it. That particular program conducted interviews the final week of the internship, and everyone knew whether or not they were welcome back at Google before they returned to school. This further exacerbated my embarrassment.

Immediately upon arriving in Boston, I updated my resume to

reflect my internship experience. I was assuming that a full-time job at Google was unlikely and wanted to be prepared. I began applying for jobs and scheduling interviews, my confidence shaken from the lack of an offer in hand. Fortunately, I was amazed when the recruiter calls and emails began pouring in. The only thing that had changed on my resume was a three-month stint at Google. Was the experience that powerful to other employers? Evidently it was.

In the meantime, I was also rigorously preparing for my Google interviews. I had already completed two interviews during the week between my internship and returning to class. I had interviewed with my potential future boss, who had begun her term as Google's Automotive Industry Director just after I departed, and I also spoke with her supervisor. Both were phone calls, which I always find are a bit trickier as you cannot see one's facial expressions. I had actually enjoyed both discussions, but my third and final conversation was to be with a Vice President at 4:00pm on a Friday afternoon. I was nervous. He ended up starting the interview a half hour late, which made me even more nervous. I managed to keep calm and carry on, but I could not gauge his reaction to my answers over the phone.

Most people in business school tend to manage stress through heavy drinking on the weekends. However, being the true nerd that I am, I handle stress by cleaning, hitting the gym, and playing the cello. Thus, after my last Google interview concluded, I prepared for my Saturday cello lesson at the New England Conservatory, packed my gym bag for the next day, and thought about other companies to pursue while cleaning my dorm room.

That last interview with Google was in the beginning of September. I finally received an offer letter in October. A wave of relief washed over me when Human Resources shared the news. Once it was signed, I immediately cancelled all of my remaining interviews and sent regrets to others who had extended me offers. I was taking a significantly smaller salary by joining Google versus many other options, and yet I was ecstatic. Cultural fit was truly far more important to me than salary.

If my fellow interns and I had sat back and accepted Human Resources' original position, we may never have had careers at Google. The path Human Resources created did not lead me to where I wanted to go; thus, I had to chart my own course. If you really want something in life, do not allow anyone to tell you it cannot be done. Create your own path and go after it.

CREATE QUICK WINS

The first day on a new job is usually a nerve-wracking experience. There are doubts about competency, future career potential, and even survival. But a true leader can capture that nervous energy and turn it into excitement, which will jump-start an individual's career more than anything. When managers take the time to set up their new employees to earn quick wins, they are helping the employees accelerate both confidence and performance. I have had the contrasting experiences of being completely abandoned as a new employee and being set up for success as a new employee. The difference is dramatic and proved to me the absolute necessity of establishing opportunities for new employees to quickly prove themselves, or creating quick wins.

My contrasting experiences began with my work at an automaker. I had spent a fantastic summer as an intern with an automaker during my junior year of college. It had been a phenomenal experience, and my boss at the time was someone I still admire to this day. In fact, he later wrote a letter of recommendation for my graduate school applications. As a result, I was full of excitement when I received a full-time offer from the automaker and returned to work there after graduation.

Unfortunately, my enthusiasm was quickly squashed when I first reported to my office. My boss had known of my arrival and start date for quite some time, but he scheduled a vacation for my first week on the job. He had assigned a fellow teammate to be my guide. However, unknown to me at the time, he had also divulged to her personal information about me, including my salary. This particular teammate was earning a lower salary than me due to differences in our education and experiences, and she did not accept that well. I was unaware of the grudge she had developed against me.

Ignorant to her bias against me and eager to please, I listened to

every word she said. I carefully followed her instructio
when I was thrown a major customer problem, I soug
advice before taking action. I followed her recommend,
which seemed in line with corporate policy but also not
understanding of the customer's circumstances, and was met
with extreme outrage by the customer on the phone. My hands
trembled as I put down the receiver. The customer's fury had
rattled me. I began to relay my story to the eavesdropping team
that had surrounded me. My "mentor" sat directly across from
me and laughed. I suddenly realized that I had been setup to
fail, and I later discovered the reason she had despised me from
the beginning. No one else knew she had guided me through
this disaster, and I held my tongue. She had fooled me, but I
would not let her embarrass me further in an office argument.
From then on, I took my training into my own hands and taught
myself everything I needed to know. If I was going to fail, it was
going to be on my terms, not anyone else's.

Consequently, despite my amazing internship experience at
Google, I was skeptical when I returned as a full-time employee.
I had been an intern with the automaker before I joined them full-
time, and I had an incredible internship experience there as well.
Yet I was terribly disappointed when I later returned. Would the
same thing happen now that I was back at Google?

My stomach was filled with fear as I returned to the Southern
California Google office for the first day of my full-time
employment. The entire Automotive team was out that day for
an event, and most of the other teams were away at client
meetings. I was greeted by a kind administrative assistant, who
showed me my desk but had no knowledge of my arrival that
day. Most new employees at the time started immediately in
Mountain View for a welcoming, corporate paperwork, etc. I had
not been instructed to do so given my internship experience, but
it seemed there was a lack of communication between Human
Resources and the office staff. The administrative assistant
showed me where I was supposed to sit, but my phone had not
even been connected yet. He gave me a copy of the *Wall Street*

Journal to keep me busy for the day.

Could this really be happening? Was this the automaker all over again?

Nervous thoughts raced through my mind and my stomach churned with anxiety when my personal cell phone rang. It was my boss, who was based in Detroit, Michigan, at the time. She immediately apologized, as she had been in touch with the Southern California Google office and learned of the disastrous set up. But she did more than that. She got me excited by outlining a few projects she wanted me to begin immediately that would quickly give me exposure to the Automotive team across the nation and allow me to prove my worth. She specifically shared that she wanted me to get "quick wins" to establish myself and build momentum for my career, and then surprised me even more by sharing that she was flying across the country next week to meet with me in person. And suddenly my fears began to dissolve.

I was immediately re-energized and motivated to succeed. I felt that this woman truly cared about my success, and was doing everything possible to ensure I had a strong start. I wanted to maximize this opportunity and hit the ground running. I was so inspired by her caring that I completed the projects successfully and early, and quickly moved on to accomplish more for the team.

I embodied these same ideals when I later lead my own team. I traveled to meet new employees immediately and always had projects planned ahead that they could quickly accomplish to gain confidence and trust from others. A little preparation and effort from a manager in the beginning can make a world of difference to a new employee. Create opportunities for your team to earn quick wins, and you will be astounded by how quickly they flourish in return.

OWN YOUR BRAND

One of my former managers at Google often told me, "Perception is reality." She believed that the way people see you is the reality they feel, and though their perception could be completely wrong, that is in fact their reality and it is your responsibility to address it. I used to think that if you led by example and always did the right thing, you would not have to worry about how people perceived you. Unfortunately, I learned that is not always true. People can perceive you incorrectly for a variety of reasons that you cannot control. Luckily, I also discovered that you can correct their misguided perceptions but only if you make the effort to own your brand.

Despite having had a successful internship and earning some impressive quick wins with the team when I returned full-time, I felt a great deal of pressure to prove myself at Google as a full-time employee. I did not want to assume that everyone knew what I was capable of. I was working hard, which I expected, but I was also traveling constantly, which I had not expected. I had anticipated traveling about once per month, but instead I was on the road every week.

I did not especially love traveling for work, as the daily work piled up during each excursion and required long nights to finish. Nevertheless, I decided to make the best of it. I had met so many amazing people at the Harvard Business School who were scattered all over the world after graduation. Luckily for me, most of the time when I traveled somewhere, I knew someone from Harvard who lived there. I tried to meet up with a former classmate on each trip in an effort to keep from getting completely lost in work.

Visiting old friends made the travels much more bearable and even exciting. A few months into the job, I had made the best of a challenging situation and was pleased with my performance thus far. On a rare morning when I was not traveling and in the

Southern California office, I bumped into my former internship boss while getting some tea.

We had not properly caught up since my full-time return to Google. She shared her latest projects with me and I told her about my constant travels. But then she caught me off guard. She asked if I was getting tired.

I had only been back for a few months. I did not want to be known as the tired, whining employee! I had shared my travel stories simply because that what I was up to. Did she think I was venting about working too much? I had to change this perception fast.

I quickly switched gears and elaborated about all of the great personal experiences I had during my travels, especially getting to catch up with old friends. I saw the expression on her face change into a big smile as she said, "Oh, good, you're having fun then!" I felt a wave of relief rush through me. I wanted nothing but positivity to kick of my career at Google, and I had almost become known for negativity without meaning to!

Since then, I have paid extra attention to people's reactions to things I say to ensure they did not misinterpret me. There are times when people will misunderstand you, but you can correct that. Your reputation and your image amount to your brand. You need to manage and control your brand just as you would a company's most valuable product. Do not let incorrect perceptions create your reputation. Own your brand and let people know who you really are and what you stand for.

CONFRONT YOUR PROBLEMS

It has always been a challenge for me to confront my professional peers. It is especially difficult in a place like Google where you are required to obtain peer evaluations which will impact your performance review. However, it is impossible to be a true leader without the ability to tackle issues with your peers head on. As a result, I forced myself to get over that uncomfortable feeling and immediately deal with problems at hand.

I was faced with such a dilemma shortly after I began my Industry Analyst role at Google. As I studied our business, I discovered a weakness in our educational outreach efforts. We wanted to familiarize local automotive dealerships with our product offerings. There were thousands and thousands of automotive dealerships scattered across the United States at the time. We had a lean team of four people tasked with this massive effort of educating dealers. They were traveling non-stop to trade shows and automotive events. They were great at connecting with individual dealers and educating them, but their efforts simply were not scalable.

I knew from my days at the automaker that dealerships needed a simple training program they could follow at their own pace within their own facility. I also felt that we as Google were not leveraging our own products in our educational efforts. I thought we could create a series of short educational videos and host them on YouTube. I ran the idea by my boss and the head of the dealer team, and they liked it. I proceeded to work with the head of the dealer team to create and produce the videos, and soon we had our own educational series live on YouTube.

The series was a big hit, and we quickly reached over 20,000 views with little promotion. The feedback from dealers was outstanding. In addition, all of the Google Automotive teams found use for the videos with other types of automotive clients beyond dealerships. The series got so much attention that other Googlers outside of the Automotive team began inquiring about our work. In fact, the Industry Marketing Managers (those who ran all marketing efforts for each of Google's Industry Teams) wanted to hear about it during our upcoming monthly Industry Management Team meeting. Unfortunately, our Automotive Industry Marketing Manager did not relay this news to me and ask me if I would be willing to present. Instead, he decided he would make the presentation himself. I did not even know it was on the upcoming meeting agenda until I got an email from him asking me questions about the program as he was going to be talking about it.

While I was thrilled that the program had gotten so much attention, I could not understand why our Industry Marketing Manager was presenting instead of me. He had nothing to do with the program whereas I had led it from conception to execution. We were both regular attendees at the meeting, so there was no reason for him to present on my behalf. These presentation opportunities were rare but important at Google, as employees were responsible for making themselves and their work known to others. I felt it was completely inappropriate for him to present on my behalf and I decided to confront him.

I responded to his email and answered all of his questions, but I also let him know that in the future I wanted to be involved in any such presentation given my familiarity with the program. He quickly replied via email and made it clear that he did not appreciate my desire to present. I was not about to get into an email war, but I needed our Industry Marketing Manager to understand my perspective. I deserved the right to own my work all the way through. I do not like things to fester, so I called him immediately.

He instantly took a defensive approach as if I were taking something away from him. He said sometimes our boss would have to present work we had done. I could have easily taken his reaction personally, but I removed emotions and stayed focused on my main objectives. I explained that while that was true, he was not my boss. We were both attendees, and given my extensive involvement in the project and his complete lack of involvement, I would expect to be involved in any such future presentations. He suddenly became flustered and backed out of the presentation completely.

I had stood my ground and took full ownership of the presentation with no regrets. If I had stepped aside and let him present my work, it would have reflected poorly upon me. People would have wondered why I was not speaking, and they would have either questioned my involvement in the project or assumed I had a fear of public speaking. It is tough to confront a peer, especially when you know he or she may not react well. I could have asked my boss to intervene, but that would have just demonstrated immaturity on my part. I faced my fear, tackled the problem head on, and then moved on. It is never easy to confront a peer, but staying focused on the main concern and avoiding emotions makes it much easier.

TALK TO PEOPLE

In a world where it is much easier to communicate with others all across the world, it is also much more important that we take the time to actually *talk* to people. Not just hide behind a screen to send an email, text, or have an online chat, but speak to someone in a conversation where you cannot stop to edit your sentence. You need to be able to conduct a real conversation, where you must listen intently and react quickly. I made a big mistake my first year at Google by hiding behind screens and other people, and I learned that is no way to make a name for yourself. Sometimes you have to put aside technology and make it a point to talk to people.

Despite my strong business skills and industry knowledge, I lacked confidence when I first joined Google full-time. Talking about your achievements was considered bragging amongst my family, and I believed that my work would speak for itself. I was essentially an introvert. The team I was joining, however, consisted of extroverts. One of them had worked for Google since before the company became public. He had worked his way up through the various sales positions to become the Automotive Industry Operations Manager. He had studied theater in college and his bold personality loved performing for an audience. He was not afraid to brag about his strong connections throughout the company, including our boss, the Automotive Industry Director.

At the time, our Industry Director was based in Michigan, our Operations Manager was based in New York, and I was based in Southern California. The Automotive Operations Manager shared many personal interests with our Industry Director, including a fascination of New York City, high end fashion, and shopping sample sales. I had absolutely zero interest in any of these things, but rather preferred the beach, sports and music. I was intimidated during their conversations as I feared my boss would find me boring. This only augmented my introverted tendencies.

The majority of the work the Automotive Operations Manager and I were each assigned to complete required us to collaborate regularly. I enjoyed working with him as he had an entertaining character and a true desire to help our team. It seemed like a natural fit to allow him to take the lead presenting our materials to our boss given his personality. I knew he would never take credit for something I had done. I failed to realize, though, that by constantly putting him center stage I was not positioning myself as a leader. I had always assumed that my work would speak for itself. But the truth is that I was creating a perception of myself as the quiet worker bee that could produce amazing projects, not someone who could not motivate an audience or team.

It took me about a year before I realized the predicament I had gotten myself into. I was attending an internal conference along with our Industry Director and Operations Manager, and there was a debate about a new way to analyze data. I had reservations about the process but I had already discussed them with my boss and thus did not feel a need to speak up in public. Afterward, she pulled me aside and mentioned that she had been waiting for me to speak up and share my thoughts with others during the debate, but I had not. I then began to evaluate how I interacted with others at meetings, conversations, and so forth, to discover that I had developed a terrible tendency to stay quiet and work behind the scenes. I communicated with my boss mostly over email and never called her without scheduling a phone meeting first.

I began to force myself to speak out in meetings and conversations. It felt incredibly awkward at first, but I pushed on. I still had a long way to go to demonstrate my capabilities but I did not want to waste another year proving myself. I needed to make a change fast.

And that is when I decided to do the simplest but scariest thing. I picked up the phone. I called my boss without a scheduled meeting notice, and just talked to her about important business issues at hand. All along I had a fear of bothering my boss and wasting her precious time. But the truth was I had insight that she needed and wanted, and it was my responsibility to share it. Once we got into the business discussion, my fears faded and I even began to have fun. I love driving business strategy and for once I was able to show it.

That little phone call was the catalyst for a major change in my behavior at Google. I found a way to be impactful and bold while still being myself. I did not need to have a big, loud personality to make a difference. I just needed to be able to talk to people. I still had a lot of work to do to build my confidence, but I was not going to hide behind the Operations Manager or a screen any longer. In addition to reaching out to my boss, I started calling other peers and managers throughout the Google Automotive business across the country. I wanted them to feel that I understood them and could support their needs. I continued to regularly call them along with my boss, and I knew their perception of me was changing as they began to reach out to me directly instead of sending requests through our Operations Manager.

No matter how outstanding your work is, if you cannot talk to others about it, they will never have a true understanding of your capabilities. It is possible to share ideas and bold thoughts without bragging and appearing arrogant. People cannot get to know you or your potential if you always let someone else represent you or if you hide behind a screen. Talk to people and show them who you really are.

STUDY OTHER LEADERS

A lot of people rely on their managers to create a course of personal development for them, but I believe this is ultimately an individual's responsibility. Of course, guidance from a manager should always be taken into consideration, but at the end of the day you are responsible for your own growth. Thus, while I worked as an Industry Analyst, I took it upon myself to learn as much as possible about managing teams at Google. I could not depend upon my boss alone to prepare me for the next level. Throughout my developmental process, I found the most effective teaching method for me was to study the company's great leaders.

Google offered many courses for managers in leadership and management, but unfortunately I was not eligible to take them since I was not technically a manager. No one directly reported to me at the time. However, I knew that in order to achieve my ultimate goal of becoming a team manager at Google, I needed to have a deeper understanding of successful leadership at the company. Google is a place where it is imperative that a manager can maintain the company culture, not just achieve revenue goals.

I was open with my boss about my long-term goals from the beginning of my career, and she advised me to find a mentor. There was not a formal company mentoring program back then, but she suggested I seek out a manager whom I greatly admired and wanted to be like. She shared that she had personally found a director she wanted to be like, established a strong relationship with her, and learned as much as possible about her work. This seemed like sound advice, but I struggled to find one manager whose style I wanted to completely imitate. Instead, I found there were certain pieces of each person that I admired, and these characteristics combined would allow me to manage in a way that was true to me.

While I knew that managers would be open to speaking with me, I wanted to be respectful of their time. I also wanted to see them in action as opposed to just hearing their ideas. Thus, I made myself available to do all the extra annoying tedious work that their teams needed but did not have the time to do. I completed extra data analyses for managers who needed help figuring out their sales quota. I partnered with another manager to create a quarterly newsletter for clients, spending painstaking hours making sure fonts and colors were perfect and text accurately aligned. I joined client calls and played the role of a scapegoat when a team had a client frustrated with our company's policies. In other words, I volunteered to do as much dirty work as possible.

Most of the work was mind-numbing, but in return I got a chance to witness managers in action under high-pressure situations. I saw how managers kept their teams positive when faced with daunting quotas. I witnessed managers extend themselves creatively to get clients to actually absorb and understand critical information that could be easily confused. Sometimes I faced managers who cracked under pressure and then had to pick themselves up in front of their teams. Other times I saw managers make promises I knew they could not deliver to both their teams and clients. Sometimes learning what *not* to do is even more important than learning what *to* do. Perhaps what surprised me the most throughout my observations was how much people needed positive reinforcement for their work, no matter how senior they were. People wanted to know they were valuable and making strong contributions. I knew everyone wanted to feel important, but I had not realized how much they really craved this type of feedback.

In the end, I found myself having stronger relationships with all of the managers I assisted. I had created a network of people more senior than myself that I could consult with and learn from. I was especially glad that I could contribute to their needs while learning myself. But most importantly, I had taken the initiative to lead my own personal development and had become a stronger leader as a result.

You can in fact learn greater concepts and push your personal development beyond your daily job with a little extra effort. The things I learned from working first-hand with the managers were lessons I could not have absorbed in a classroom or from a book. Take the time to study other leaders, learn from them, and then create a style that best suits you.

BEWARE OF INSECURITY

Throughout my career at Google, I was always fascinated by the people I encountered. My fellow colleagues all had such incredible and diverse backgrounds, and I loved learning from them. Unfortunately, despite their phenomenal skillsets and talents, there were still some people who felt insecure. And insecurity, I soon realized, can be detrimental to a team and bring out the worst in people. Thus, I discovered rather quickly the importance of recognizing when someone else was feeling insecure and how to avoid the dangers these feelings could cause.

Google is a place where collaboration is *strongly encouraged* and putting others down to promote yourself is *strongly discouraged*. However, insecure people sometimes strive to embarrass others. They have a need to make themselves feel better and for some reason the only way they think they can do that is by making someone else look bad. When I first joined Google, I was in awe of the amazing people I worked with. I had tremendous respect for my peers and their knowledge. As a result, I was in shock and dismay when I encountered Googlers who reacted badly to me simply because I possessed an MBA degree from the Harvard Business School.

Although I was incredibly proud of my MBA as it had been no small feat to achieve this degree, I went through great lengths to avoid speaking about my Harvard experience. I was aware that it could intimidate others even when that was not my intention; thus, I did not make references to my educational background unless specifically asked. My team was of course aware of my background as were several others throughout the company (news and gossip spread fast) but it was despite my efforts to keep a low profile.

Nevertheless, insecure people often found a way to bring up the topic of my education with hidden insults. Early in my career, I

28

attended an internal leadership conference with senior sales management. There was a dinner during the conference in which employees were assigned to a specific table with various senior leaders. The goal was to help us network and learn from great leaders we did not have the opportunity to work with on a regular basis. I happened to be assigned to a rather intimidating table, including a global sales leader, my boss' supervisor, and the most Senior Industry Director at the time. A few other employees who were the same level as me also joined the table, including a man that had been part of my internship class at Google. The former intern and my boss' supervisor were the only ones who knew I held an MBA from Harvard.

The former intern also possessed an MBA, but from a public university that was not especially known for its MBA program. The Senior Industry Director was one of the few Industry Directors who did not hold a graduate degree, though he had extraordinary work experience. Both of these men were known for holding a grudge against Ivy League graduates. During the middle of dinner, the former intern mentioned an article he had recently read highlighting the fact that more major companies had CEOs who graduated from public universities as opposed to CEOs who had graduated from private schools. He looked directly at me with a wicked smile as he began the conversation, and I instantly knew where this was headed.

As expected, the Senior Industry Director pounced in at the opportunity to bash Ivy League graduates. He began to complain how it was impossible to meet a Harvard Business School graduate who could not wait more than a minute to "drop the H-bomb," or reveal that he or she had attended Harvard. He went on to ridicule the attitude and arrogance of Harvard graduates, and was constantly egged on by the former intern.

My blood was boiling and I stirred uncomfortably in my seat. The only arrogant people I sensed at this table were not Ivy League graduates, but rather the Director and the former intern. I knew

Harvard graduates who could barely pay back their student loans because they wanted to work for non-profit firms and make a difference in the world. And instead of sitting with those inspiring classmates, I was stuck watching two insecure men commiserate and despair about how horrible Harvard graduates were? I wanted to jump out of my seat and start a tirade about how ignorant they really were.

But that is exactly what the former intern wanted me to do. He wanted me to make a fool of myself. He had been trying to compete with me ever since we were interns. He did not realize, though, that I recognized his insecurity. I was not going to fall for it. I held my tongue and did not say a word until there was an opportunity to change the conversation, and then I immediately jumped in on a new topic.

I could feel my boss' supervisor watching me throughout the conversation, waiting to see how I would respond. We ended up developing a strong working relationship and I became his key advisor for anything related to Industry Analysts. I believe he respected my ability to stay above the fray and avoid unnecessary conflict. Ironically, the former intern worked in the same office as this senior leader in New York, and yet I was the one who held the strong relationship despite working across the country and rarely seeing him in person.

It would have been very easy for me to jump and attack the Senior Industry Director and the former intern for their absurdity, but it would have only hurt me. I wanted to maintain a professional reputation, and a true leader knows better than to fall prey to someone else's insecurity. Beware of insecure people who are knowingly trying to bring you down and simply avoid their pitiful traps. You will demonstrate your true integrity to others by staying objective and focused on the business instead of engaging in a personal battle.

PROTECT YOUR TEAM

Googlers took a great deal of pride in their work, but nevertheless there were still times when a team failed to meet its goals. While most teams quickly bounced back from a loss, there was occasionally a group that needed more help and required intervention from senior management. I observed that in such times of trouble, the team manager absolutely must protect his or her team or else the team is doomed for failure.

When I worked as an Industry Analyst for Google's Automotive vertical, we had one particular team that was dedicated exclusively to one client, whereas all the other teams managed multiple clients. They had more staff than any of our other Automotive teams, though we all agreed that was appropriate for such a demanding client. Yet they continuously struggled to meet their sales quotas and other goals. As an Industry Management Team, we began to dig deeper into this business segment in an effort to find ways we could further assist. We thought we could aid the team by creating additional analyses, taking on extra client meetings and calls, anything to lighten their load so they could drive the business forward.

Our efforts were met with strong resistance, which started with the team manager. She was not solutions-oriented, and rather than focus on what could be done, she preferred to complain about her client's bureaucratic structure and how difficult it was for the client to make a decision. Her negativity drowned her team as well. When we spoke to her team about the business, they were quick to blame Google for not offering better systems to support the client's demands.

We worked with each individual on that team to try and adopt a solutions-oriented approach, but the team was struggling to get past its manager's attitude. With our open floor setup, everyone could hear her repeatedly complain about the client to her team instead of brainstorm alternative possibilities. Eventually the poor performance continued to a point where senior management called for a business review.

The review was to be led by a Regional Sales Director who asked that the Industry Management Team attend the review to offer our industry expertise as needed. The review was intended to have direct and if necessary harsh conversations about the business. Thus, it was expected but not explicitly stated that only the team manager would attend. Instead, she brought her entire team along with her to the meeting. My heart sank when I saw them all sitting in the room. I knew this review would crush any morale they had left.

The manager had her team create and present a slideshow on the state of the business. The Regional Sales Director picked apart the flawed analysis and our Operations Manager aggressively attacked it as well. I saw many problems in the presentation, but I could not call them out. I did not believe the team deserved that. The manager did, but not her team. She had set them up for failure and blame. She should have been the scapegoat and spared her team this embarrassment.

As an Industry Management Team, we were all furious that the manager had pulled in her entire team. But we had erred, too. We should have confirmed with the Regional Sales Director and the manager that this was in fact just a review with the manager. We should not have assumed she would come alone. The truth is that we failed to protect her team just as much as she did. Needless to say, that team as it stood was never able to recover. The manager eventually left the company and once a new manager was in place the team slowly found its momentum.

A true leader will protect his or her team and take responsibility when things are going badly. A true leader knows that is the only way to gain trust and move forward. I never forgot what it felt like to watch that team squirm in embarrassment during the business review. Later when I led my own team, I was always the first one to take the heat when there was trouble. Never leave your team to take the blame. Stand strong and demonstrate that you will protect them. Otherwise, you will look like a coward and no one can respect someone like that as a leader.

BE TRANSPARENT

Sometimes leaders have to keep things quiet in order to protect the best interests of their company. But once a decision has been implemented, it is absolutely critical to communicate to all stakeholders and be transparent about the desired result. Otherwise, people will commence unproductive speculation which can lead to fear. I watched this dramatically unfold when a Googler in our regional office was let go from the company.

It is beyond uncomfortable to have a fellow peer fired, even when the situation demands no other alternative. Early in my career at Google, a peer from the Automotive team was released while I was on vacation. I was not surprised by the news as I had encountered many of his performance issues first-hand. However, I was astounded by how much the rest of the office began speculating the cause of his departure. His core team knew the real reasons, as did I since I worked so closely with them, but the remainder of the sales force in the office did not understand. They had not worked side by side with him, but rather just enjoyed his presence in the café, at company social functions, and at volunteer activities.

I had been notified about the situation while I was on vacation, and had assumed the office gossip would have died down by the time I was back in the office. Instead, immediately upon my return people began quizzing me for details about the employee's departure. My fellow Googlers viewed me as a possible new source of information. But I refused to leak the story. Some members of the Automotive team explained to me how frustrated they felt with our office peers pushing for information. I shared their annoyance, as it seemed people were being too nosy. We had so much work to do, how did anyone have time to focus on this?

But later I realized that our peers were acting out of fear. No one had shared with them the details of why the employee had been let go. They likely wanted to make sure they did not end up in a similar fate. They had seen a fun, caring guy in the office, but had no idea of what his actual performance was like. They likely would not have been so fearful if they had a better understanding of the performance issues that took place. Instead of gossiping and being unproductive, they could have focused on their work. There are of course limits to what information can and cannot be shared in such situations, but in retrospect I imagine a town hall meeting or individual team meetings would have made a big difference in this instance.

However, it was not just management who lacked transparency in this situation. My Automotive peers and I never shared our frustrations with management. We could have asked for the office leaders to address the situation. Instead, we sulked quietly and complained to each other. We should have been vocal about our concerns and transparent in our need for help. We were equally to blame.

This situation taught me the dangerous and unintentional consequences that can occur if you are not transparent. It is important to think beyond the core team that can be impacted by a decision to include all possible stakeholders. Communicating as much as possible with these stakeholders can mitigate fear and unproductive gossip. It can also protect those who are most impacted by a change. At the same time, if you are feeling challenged by a situation, you have a responsibility to be open and honest about your concerns to management. If management is unaware of a problem, it is impossible for them to help you. Be transparent as much as possible, and everyone will have a better understanding of what is expected of them.

CREATE CONFIDENCE

A professor at the Harvard Business School once shared with our class an idea that most people are motivated by fear, particularly fear of failure. I kept this thought with me over the years, and in fact I have observed that even the most senior leaders often long for a supporting voice to boost their confidence. I myself struggled with confidence in the workplace despite my strong credentials, until I found a way to weave in my personal passion with my professional work.

One of the things I especially enjoyed at Google was learning about Googlers' passions outside of the office. Everyone seemed to have hidden talents and discovering them made me feel like I was constantly enriching my life through learning. Google put forth great efforts to stimulate personal interests as well; a wise move as happy employees tend to be much more productive than unhappy ones. There were email groups and clubs to encourage communication amongst those with similar interests, including topics such as music, sports, parenthood, beauty, travel, and more. Even our little office in Southern California encouraged creativity. I experienced this first-hand as my fellow Googlers supported my passion for the cello.

I began playing the cello in the sixth grade, and it quickly became an integral part of my life. I was excited to share my love of music with my fellow Googlers as I had learned during my internship how appreciative they were of each other's talents. I felt so comfortable revealing this part of myself to my co-workers that I even changed my online internal company profile picture to a photo of myself holding the cello.

I was amazed by how much attention people actually noticed this profile picture. My colleagues across the country saw this picture whenever they looked up my name to find my corporate contact information, and it was an instant conversation starter. "I saw your profile pic. How long have you been playing for?" This in turn made it comfortable for me to ask my peers about their personal hobbies as well. These short conversations were actually incredibly important. They lead me to view my peers not just as colleagues but as fascinating people, which made them even more fun to work with.

However, my peers were not the only ones who paid attention to my musical interests. I was fortunate to have a boss who had an appreciation for the arts, and she often inquired about my musical talents. She repeatedly asked when I would play for the team. Performing for my peers was one thing, but for my boss? Just the idea sent nervous chills up my spine. I managed to brush off the idea for quite a few months as our team was scattered across the country.

But in June 2008, we would all be together at the annual sales conference. And a big feature of the sales conference happened to be a Googler talent show. My boss wanted the Automotive team to be represented in the talent show, and she immediately approached me about performing. The idea terrified me, but I had to remain composed before my Industry Director. The conference was not local for me and I needed to travel by plane to attend. I told her I was grateful for her thinking of me, which I was. "I would love to perform, but then I would have to buy a plane ticket for my cello. I can't risk damaging it as checked luggage," I added, thinking that would immediately kill the idea. On the contrary, I was stunned as she responded without hesitation, "So buy a ticket."

I think my heart may have stopped for a few seconds as my face froze in disbelief. I managed to quickly pull myself together and make sure I heard her correctly. There was no mistake and no backing out. I now had to prepare not only to play for the entire Automotive team, but for all of Google USA's sales and marketing staff! I had performed semi-professionally as a soloist countless times up until that point, including intense state competitions. But this performance would impact my

37

professional reputation. Google's most senior sales staff would be in attendance up to the Vice President level. I was absolutely mortified.

Despite my intense preparation, my nerves continued to unravel as the performance neared. Never before had I allowed my personal and professional lives intertwine so much, and I feared I had made a devastating mistake. *What if I bomb the performance? How will I ever face my colleagues? What will my boss think of me?* The doubts in my mind continued to snowball up until a few minutes before the show.

I could not eat anything the day of the talent show, which is extremely rare for me. Everyone I saw at the sales conference shared their excitement for my performance, further exacerbating my shakiness. We had a big team meeting just before the show and it took every last ounce of strength just to maintain my composure and concentration. I held my hands in my lap under the table to hide my trembling fingers. My boss addressed the team in closing statements, and just as I was about to breathe a sigh of relief that the meeting was over, she began to discuss the talent show.

She addressed how our Automotive team would be well-represented this year thanks to my performance, and she made it clear to me that all would be cheering me on. I was humbled by her words, but that was not all. Another auto colleague from our New York office then entered the room with a giant poster board featuring my enlarged company profile picture (with the cello) and the words "We ♥ Linda. Go Auto!!" printed below. The entire auto team had their own individual poster of me to carry in the crowd.

There were tears in my eyes as I looked around the room and felt everyone's support. The team was genuinely thrilled about my performance and wanted me to do well. They believed in me. They had no doubt I would shine on stage. It made me realize that it was time to start believing in myself.

I was still a little shaky backstage, but a rush of confidence came over me as I heard my teammates chanting my name from the audience. I took the stage with a big smile and zoned out to the music. I had created a slideshow of funny team photos which played on giant screens next to me during the performance, and my heart soared as I heard the audience laugh along. I will never forget their thunderous applause when I concluded and bowed. However, the biggest honor for me was when my boss hugged me afterward and said, "I am so proud of you."

In hindsight, that musical performance began a major turning point for my professional career. Senior managers and directors who I had previously had to re-introduce myself to at each meeting suddenly remembered my name. It became easy to speak with them and voice my opinion in large groups. I stopped worrying about what people would think if I was wrong. I had finally developed genuine confidence in myself. Later when I became a manager myself, I made extra effort to know my team's personal interests and incorporate them into our work on a regular basis. Whether it was their love of reading, a school football team, or dancing, I found ways to let them share their passions with the team on a regular basis. It took our team communications to a higher level, where people were more comfortable and consequently more confident to share big ideas and different thinking. Help your team members create confidence by supporting their personal passions, and you will be impressed by their resulting growth and creative contributions.

NEVER STOP LEARNING

One of my favorite career activities is educating others through public speaking, but I was not always very good at it. I spent a great deal of time practicing, studying speakers I admired, and even attending classes. I improved tremendously as a result of my efforts, but I was surprised to encounter senior leaders on a similar educational journey. I was inspired by them as they demonstrated you should never stop learning.

While I was often shy to play my cello in front of a crowd, I was surprisingly not intimidated by public speaking. Perhaps this is because I was always confident in the material I was presenting as I studied it thoroughly until I felt like a subject matter expert. Nevertheless, I knew that confidence and topic expertise were not enough to be a motivating speaker. I wanted to learn how to engage with an audience, how to navigate tricky questions, and how to keep an audience captive instead of boring them to death. I was fortunate that Google offered several courses regarding public speaking, and I signed up for all that I could.

The first class was hosted in my regional office, and it left me feeling quite embarrassed. It focused on the tone of our voice, and the analysis of how we spoke was somewhat musical. As a cellist, I found it fascinating. As a speaker, I was dismayed to hear the recordings of myself. I sounded like an annoying cartoon character! Everyone in the class had their own personal struggles and was incredibly supportive of each other. But I was still ashamed of my vocal recordings given my perfectionist tendencies.

Thus, I was a little apprehensive about attending my next class, and I needed to travel to San Francisco for it. Instead of being surrounded by local office buddies, I was in a room with complete strangers. And they were not just peers. There were managers and even a Senior Industry Director in the class. I had heard these leaders speak publicly before, and I could not fathom that they needed classes. I wondered what they were doing there.

My astonishment continued as the class instructor paired off the students to give each other feedback, and I was assigned to work with the Senior Industry Director. My stomach filled with nervous butterflies. I had no idea how I could give him helpful feedback. He knew so much more than I did! But as the class went on, I realized that I did in fact have something to contribute. He not only welcomed my feedback, but he encouraged it and accepted it graciously. I was able to share some thoughts that he later included during an actual presentation.

That class taught me a lot more than just how to become a better public speaker. It taught me that everyone always has something to learn, and everyone always has something to teach, no matter what level he or she may be. I was inspired by the humble Senior Industry Director who was striving to learn more despite always appearing so confident in public, and I was also surprised to discover that I could teach him something new despite my lack of experience. As a result, I have always made it known to my peers, managers, and employees that I am especially excited to learn from them. You should never stop learning as there is always room for improvement.

AVOID THE GOSSIP

There was one downside to the close-knit culture at Google. Sometimes gossip could run rampant from office to office and create a serious distraction. At times it felt a little bit like high school. It was easy to get caught up in the rumors as things were constantly changing at Google and people thought inside information might help them stay ahead of the game. However, I learned that it was better to steer clear of the gossip and remain focused on the work at hand.

The continuous changes at Google and in the marketplace meant there were times the company needed to re-organize its sales and marketing teams. I was working as an Industry Analyst the first time I experienced reorganization at Google. I felt suspicious as I began receiving numerous internal data requests regarding our industry's performance from senior management. My fellow Automotive Operations Manager was also inundated with similar requests. We felt anxious as we knew something would happen based on the data, but we had no idea what.

Google's open culture meant that anyone could access anyone else's corporate calendar and see what meetings they had planned. Googlers soon began stalking managers' calendars and gossiping about their meetings. Rumors began to spread like wildfire and the office atmosphere became incredibly tense.

It did not take long before everyone began to anticipate reorganization, but apprehension increased as people began to fear layoffs. It became terribly difficult to have a productive meeting with anyone as most people wanted to share the latest gossip. While I believe that knowledge is power and knowing the details about a situation can help you be prepared, I do not believe in speculating about corporate gossip. I found myself listening and not speaking a word throughout these conversations, and I always felt exhausted afterward. Gossip is not productive. It only instills more fear and wastes time. The rumors reached a point where even after work I was receiving phone calls just to hypothesize what was to come.

Thus, I made a conscious decision to isolate myself from the drama. I declined as many meeting notices as possible, stating that I had key deadlines to meet. I stopped answering phone calls from major gossipers. I had no idea how the reorganization would unfold, or if my job would be impacted. However, I always wanted to be known as someone who put their best foot forward no matter how stressful a situation may be. I stayed focused on the job I had at the time.

The reorganization was rather significant and many roles changed. Some people did unfortunately lose their jobs, while others were assigned more challenging positions. Many people were upset, others were thrilled. I myself ended up with double the workload of any other Industry Analyst with no increase in pay. Yet I was pleased about it as I knew the assignment demonstrated that the company recognized my abilities. I trusted that Google would reward me in the future for extra work during the present, and this was in fact true. It was a blessing to be able to trust a company so much.

While that was the first reorganization I experienced at Google, it was not my last. Nevertheless, it taught me a valuable lesson that I later shared with my direct reports when they experienced their first stressful reorganization. You cannot gain anything except fear by engaging in gossip. Stay committed to your work. If you do your job well enough, your efforts will be recognized and you will end up fine. If you cannot stay focused during times of crisis, this will demonstrate an inability to lead. By avoiding gossip you can shine through like a leader and spare yourself unnecessary stress, too.

TAKE TIME TO RECHARGE

It never seemed like there was a good time to take a vacation at Google. Things moved so fast that all of our objectives and results were measured in quarters. Taking two weeks off meant losing about 15% of the available working days in a quarter. Many employees genuinely feared that their managers would give them a lower personal score at the end of the quarter for taking off more than two weeks. However, I learned that it is absolutely necessary for you to take time to recharge. A real break from the office helps you get a fresh mind, a new level of positive energy, and increase your productivity.

There are too many studies that cite how happy employees are more productive, and I firmly believe this. I was fortunate to have a boss that supported this notion as well. Each year she would take two weeks off in the summer to travel overseas in addition to extra time around the holidays. She liked to travel overseas so that she was less accessible to the office and could really get a break. Many Googlers referred to vacation time as a "digital detox."

Before joining Google, each summer I took a big trip with my family. I vowed to keep this tradition alive despite my hectic schedule. We planned our summer adventures as early as January so I could give my colleagues sufficient notice. Scheduling vacation far in advance also enabled me to work ahead of deadlines as much as possible. I made extraordinary efforts to do more work before any trip in order to ease the burden on my peers. I wanted to honor commitments to both my team and my family.

My family had planned a three-week trip overseas for the summer of 2009. Yet less than a month before I was scheduled to fly, the company's sales and marketing reorganization happened. While I understood my new role, I still had not been assigned an official boss. Senior leadership was still interviewing and deciding who that would be. All of the Industry Analysts were a bit in limbo, myself included. A Senior Director who barely interacted with us was responsible for our quarterly performance reviews until an official manager was named.

I suddenly felt a panicked sensation spread throughout my body. Our temporary boss did not know me, my track record, or how much I had prepared in advance for this trip. She knew nothing of my work ethic other than what she had heard second-hand. I knew I had a strong reputation within the company, but I wanted to maintain it. I did not have my old boss to defend me anymore. Thus, I contemplated canceling the trip.

My brother and mother had extra time off that summer and had already begun the trip. My father delayed traveling with them so he could fly with me to meet them. Canceling the trip would have been a major disappointment to my family. I would have shown them that work was more important than they were.

But I had worked so hard to establish myself as a leader at Google. I did not want to waste all that effort for one trip, either.

I tend to get my best ideas while exercising. I logged in several hours at the gym as I struggled to make my decision. I hoped that a new manager would be named before I had to depart, so that I could meet with him or her before traveling. Unfortunately, the company was taking its time and it became clear that a new manager would not be announced before I needed to leave.

In the end, I thought about why I had joined Google in the first place. I came to Google because of its people, its company culture. This was a place where people should understand and respect a well-deserved vacation. This was a place where people should be happy to see their peers enjoying life outside of the office. And if it was not in fact that place, and my vacation would ruin everything I had worked for, then it was not the right place for me.

45

I took the trip.

It was one of the greatest decisions I have ever made. Not only did I come back refreshed, relaxed and ready to attack my challenging assignments with vigor, I was also blessed to meet my future husband that summer. A new manager was announced during the middle of my trip, which I learned through email (I did still check email probably more than I should have during vacation). I was able to make a great first impression with her when I returned thanks to my positive energy.

And so I experienced first-hand how powerful and imperative it is to take time to recharge. Everyone needs a break, and with proper preparation a vacation does not have to be detrimental to your peers. Later as a manager myself I always encouraged my team to take vacation time, but I also guided them on how to properly prepare so they could rest at ease without burdening their colleagues. Make time for yourself, and plan accordingly so you can really enjoy it instead of feeling guilty and worried. You never know, one small break could completely change your life!

GIVE EVERYONE A CHANCE

Although my favorite part about working at Google was the people, there were a few individuals I struggled to get along with. I did of course always maintain a professional relationship with everyone, but I almost missed out on an amazing friendship because I was afraid to work with someone whose boss I did not like. I luckily learned my lesson before it was too late and now I know the importance of giving everyone a chance no matter what the circumstances.

I had spent a considerable amount of time working with our Automotive Industry Marketing Manager, and unfortunately I found it extremely difficult to accomplish objectives together. While I knew he created a favorable impression for those outside of our team, I found it challenging to even carry a conversation with him. I did not feel that he respected my opinions, and I always felt that he resented me for having contradicting ideas.

I kept my thoughts to myself, but I soon learned that other esteemed leaders in the company were having similar difficulties working with this Industry Marketing Manager. There was certainly comfort in knowing I was not the only one who felt frustrated, but that did not make it any easier to work with him. After the company reorganization, our Industry Marketing Manager had an employee assigned to work directly under him, titled Industry Marketing Coordinator, and she began to interact with myself and the Automotive Industry Director more than the Industry Marketing Manager did.

Our Industry Marketing Coordinator was always polite, but I was afraid to get too close. She reported directly to the Industry Marketing Manager, and I knew if she crossed him it could be dangerous for her performance reviews. Thus, I intentionally kept my distance and tried to limit contact with our Industry Marketing Coordinator as much as possible.

Meanwhile, I was working very closely with the Automotive Industry Director, and she began to regularly praise our Industry Marketing Coordinator's efforts. I considered our Industry Director to be a strong judge of character, but I was a bit startled. The Industry Marketing Coordinator seemed to work so tightly with the Industry Marketing Manager. How was it possible that she could keep him happy and at the same time work so well with   others?

I had to find out for myself. Slowly, I began to reach out to our Industry Marketing Coordinator more often, and I stopped trying to limit our interactions. She was based in Michigan, and I made extra effort to meet with her in person whenever I visited that office. Not only did I realize she was in fact wonderful to work with, she was also an incredible person. I enjoyed collaborating with her on projects and spending time with her, and we soon became good friends. In fact, I was honored later to have her as a guest at my wedding.

To this day I regret that I did not give our Industry Marketing Coordinator a fair chance when I first met her. I never made things more complicated for her, but I did not try to make them easier, either. I wrongly judged her because she worked for someone I found difficult. She was her own person, and an amazing person at that. I am lucky that I was able to change my foolish ways before it was too late to develop a strong relationship and friendship with her. Since then, I have made it a point to give everyone a fair chance no matter what I may have heard about them. Do not miss an opportunity to interact with phenomenal people. Give everyone a chance to prove themselves.

CHALLENGE THE SYSTEM

Companies have rules and policies in place to protect all of their stakeholders, including employees. However, sometimes there is a better way to do something, and changing the rules can lead to greater growth and prosperity for all. You could actually hinder yourself and your company by staying silent when you see a flaw in the system. Going through the promotion process at Google taught me the importance of respectfully challenging a company to create a positive change.

At the time when I was an Industry Analyst, Google offered promotion cycles only twice a year. It was an extremely competitive process. The requirements included, but were not limited to, references from Senior Directors, many consecutive quarters of outstanding performance scores, peer endorsements, and a demonstrated ability to perform at the next level. Unfortunately, even if an employee met all of the required criteria, he or she was not guaranteed a promotion. There were a limited number of promotion slots available in each cycle, making the process even more competitive. A manager had to be ready to battle to get his or her employees promoted. Thus, it was common for employees to be recommended for promotion more than once before they were actually awarded one.

The major benefit of a promotion was not salary; rather, it was being graded at a higher numerical level. The level rating of employees determined eligibility for various roles within the organization. By fall of 2009, I had been an Industry Analyst for over two years. I had handled double the workload of any other Industry Analyst and taken on responsibilities well beyond my role. I had been nominated for promotion in the previous cycle and was devastated to receive a rejection. I was told I needed to share my work more and establish myself as a resource amongst my peers. In other words, my work was outstanding but no one outside of my team knew about it, and I had not built up a strong enough peer networks.

49

Sharing my work was a major challenge for me, not because I was selfish, but because I feared appearing obnoxious. I did not want to be "bragging" about my achievements. I just wanted to focus on my work and get the job done. But I was not going to miss my next chance to be promoted as I desperately wanted to move closer toward my goal of becoming a team manager. I had reached a point where my learning was limited in my current position and it was time for me to move on. I was being challenged merely by the quantity of work I had to complete, not the type of work, which left me constantly frustrated.

Thus, I made a dedicated effort to share work and grow my peer network. When the next promotion cycle came, I was confident. We had recently gone through an organizational restructuring and I had a new manager who had only known me for a short period of time, but I believed in my work and my documented performance history. My new manager was encouraging and also seemed confident about this promotion cycle for me.

And then suddenly she dealt me a shocking blow. I was no longer being considered for promotion. After the reorganization, our Analytical Team had grown massively and included a significant number of employees many levels lower than me. The Analytical Team Director wanted to promote the new members of our group because their levels were so low and they were being asked to do much higher level work than before. The challenge was that there were a limited number of promotional slots, and if the Director followed this strategy, there would not be a slot left for me.

My manager hinted at a salary increase to make it up to me, but I was not after money. I wanted to grow and be challenged, and I would lose my mind if I had to wait for another promotion cycle to possibly be promoted. My heart ached as I began to wonder if there really was a future for me at Google. I felt as if my career with the company had immediately come to a grinding halt.

50

Though I felt despaired, I was not ready to give up yet. I reached out to a trusted mentor and shared my story. She had recently become an Industry Director and was more familiar with the back end of the promotion process than myself. She graciously took it upon herself to speak with my former supervisor, who had become a Vice President during the reorganization.

Shortly after, the Vice President reached out to me directly herself. She asked if I had been given feedback regarding anything missing in my performance that would prevent a promotion, but I had not. She promised to investigate and made it clear that a rejection should come with feedback for improvement. I was no longer confident in the promotion process, but my confidence in the company was restored. If a newly-minted Vice President at the company who had an incredibly full plate to deal with could find the time to reach out to me directly about my career concerns, I knew that there was in fact a future for me at Google.

I soon learned from my manager that I was once again being considered for promotion, and shortly after that my official promotion was announced. My former boss, the Vice President, had respectfully challenged the system. As a result, I was promoted and came to work with a new rigor and dedication that certainly benefited my peers, clients, and of course Google.

I could have handled that situation by whining and complaining or I could have sulked silently and searched for other jobs outside of Google. Instead, I sought out the professional opinion of someone I trusted. Our Vice President could have ignored my problem with her busy schedule, but she took the time to understand the situation and the need for improvement. A true leader, she invested extra time in her people, and made a change to benefit all. No matter how great a company is, there is always room for improvement, and you should not be afraid to fight for the right change.

LEAD WITH PASSION, NOT EMOTION

Throughout my career and education, I have always performed better when I am doing something I love. Work without passion is simply torture. But I learned at Google that there is a fine line between leading with passion and leading with emotion. Leading with emotion can bring teams up very high during good times. However, leading with emotion during rough times can result in harsh feelings amongst teams, a loss of respect from peers, and bad decisions that cannot be forgotten. I faced these challenges head on when working for an emotional leader at Google.

One of my greatest challenges during my Google career was setting team quarterly quotas. It was more than determining the right mathematical model. People's lives were affected by the numbers we set. Their compensation was tied to how they performed against the target. If we were too aggressive, they would suffer. If we were too lenient, our peers would carry an unnecessary burden to compensate for us. We also had to incorporate uncertain qualitative intelligence from the sales teams and adjust accordingly. It was a never-ending yet crucial challenge to set fair targets.

As an Industry Analyst, I played a heavy role in this process. I scrutinized internal and external market trends, I researched industry news, and I talked to each manager individually to understand what they expected from clients. There was always a little fear inside of me, not because I doubted my skills, but because I knew how much these numbers impacted everyone else.

There was one particular quarter when a sector, which was a group of four industries at the time, was assigned a very aggressive quota. It was then up to the Sector Lead to allocate that quota across the four industries. If one team took less, another team had to take more. It also happened that during this particular quarter, for the first time I was assigned to work for two

52

industries. I was the only Analyst covering two industries, Entertainment and Automotive, who were essentially competing with each other.

I happened to be traveling in Michigan on business when the draft allocations were distributed by our Sector Lead. I had discussed quota expectations with both of my Directors, and I knew neither one would be pleased. But I did not anticipate how badly the reaction could be. The Entertainment Director was in California, and he immediately began to send me instant messages. He was outraged and on the verge of exploding. I did not know him well enough to understand what could calm him down, so instead I tried to buy myself time. I steered the conversation toward the type of data we could use to support his case. I wanted to get him focused on actions we could take as opposed to anger.

Meanwhile, it was not long before the Automotive Director began to instant message me as well. But she did something that completely caught me off guard. She gave me time and space. She sensed I was caught between the two industries. She believed in me and knew that I understood the quota process and what she needed. We agreed on a time to reconvene and then she let me be. For the first time that day, I felt that I could breathe.

I locked myself in a video conference room and went to work with our Entertainment Director. Despite my efforts to stay focused on the facts and process, he could not help but express extreme anger and frustration. I knew that he cared about his team and he wanted to do the right thing, but by being so emotional I also knew we were headed in a dangerous direction. We needed to proceed with confidence. We had no idea where the numbers would end up, and if it was an aggressive target, we had to give the teams a confident start. If they saw us panicking, they would never believe they could accomplish the goals. Google buildings have an open floorplan to encourage collaboration. There was no hiding our stress from the teams throughout the process.

I was the last one in the office that evening as I crunched away numbers, and I worked through the night back at my hotel room. I felt anxious and uneasy as I returned to the office the next day, but not because I was worried about the numbers. Rather, I feared how our Entertainment Director would react to the end result and the message it would send to the team. The emotional discussions had left me feeling utterly exhausted.

In the end, the final targets were challenging for all parties involved. Afterward, I could not help but reflect upon the leadership differences between the two directors I was working for and my own reactions to their behavior. I felt anxious under the emotional leadership, whereas I was calm and focused under the objective leadership. I realized then how important it is to lead with passion, not emotion. Leaders need to show their teams that they care and that they are willing to fight for them. However, emotional leadership can demonstrate a lack of control and unintentionally create fear. Lead with passion to inspire your teams, but keep your emotions at home.

PROVE YOURSELF

Managers today are juggling too many people and too many tasks, and it is impossible for them to really know everything you are capable of unless you show them. My managers at Google were all incredibly kind and caring people, but there were times when they really had no idea how much more I was capable of until I took it upon myself to show them. I could not wait for them to notice my talents. I had to prove myself to get where I wanted to go.

Ever since I joined Google, I knew that I wanted to manage my own team. I had specifically pursued an MBA at the Harvard Business School to prepare for a leadership role. I had plenty of experience leading people on a professional level and the analytical skills necessary to push for results. But once again I soon realized that my fellow Googlers were not fully aware of all my managerial talents and it was my responsibility to prove them.

After earning my promotion in 2009, I was ready to take on a new role. I had been leading all of the Automotive vertical's analysis efforts, and I was the only Analyst who had been responsible for more than one vertical. However, I was bored. I was challenged only by the volume of work I had to complete, not the type of work. I was anxious to lead my own team.

I shared my intentions to become a manager with my direct supervisor and Industry Director even though there were not any open roles at the time. I wanted to be top of mind when a position did open up. I wanted to become a manager so badly that I even offered to relocate for such an opening. In the meantime, I sought out volunteer opportunities within the company to further develop my skills. A local team in the Automotive Vertical, known as a pod, had become severely understaffed. Some of the pod members had taken on new roles on other teams and two of the pod's top performers were about to begin a six-month maternity leave.

I could sense the Automotive Industry Director's concern and see the team beginning to panic. I called our Industry Director and volunteered to fill in the role of Account Manager. I had no experience in the role but knew I had the skills to figure it out. The Industry Director, Pod Manager, and pod were all elated!

I was able to quickly feel comfortable in the position, and spending more time with the pod further solidified my desire to be a Pod Manager. I received no extra compensation for my work as an Account Manager and was still held to the highest standards for my responsibilities as an Industry Analyst. But I knew the value of my work. In the future as a Pod Manager I could easily support or question an Account Manager's work. Most importantly, I could earn the trust of Account Managers because I had walked in their shoes.

Then another surprise hit the California Automotive Pod. Their Pod Manager was moving on to a new position in another state. This was it, the opportunity I had been waiting for! A manager role in the location I wanted with growing clients and a fantastic team. I knew there was another strong candidate for the role, the team's current Account Executive. She had worked with all of the team's clients for several years and was an outstanding employee. But I was confident in my skill set and knew I could excel in the role as Pod Manager. I anxiously awaited the job posting details so I could apply.

Unfortunately, I was soon dealt with a horrific blow to my confidence. The Automotive Industry Director called and asked me to participate on the interview committee. In other words, *I was not even in her consideration set for the job*. I felt as if she had crushed my heart in her hand but I somehow forced myself to speak with a brave voice and graciously accepted her offer to join the committee. I was thankful she could not see the disappointment and heartbreak in my face over the phone.

I could have turned down her offer to serve on the interview committee and instead told her that I wanted to apply for the job. But I knew an interview alone would not be enough to convince her of my talents if I was not in her original consideration set. And if my own Industry Director did not consider me worthy of management, it was highly unlikely that another Industry Director would, either.

When the position was finally posted, I was bombarded by people in my office wondering if was applying for the job. My local colleagues had a better understanding of my leadership abilities. It felt like a tiny stab wound every time someone asked me open manager's position. But I carried on with a positive face, and always answered with a strong voice that I was on the interview committee, as if I was not at all interested in the role.

The current Pod Manager quickly moved into her new role before we were even halfway done with the interview process, and with the amazing Account Executive out on maternity leave, I could see a serious lack of leadership on the team. I quietly stepped in and asserted my presence as a leader. I helped the team get organized, I provided individual guidance, and I spent extra time with clients. All of this work was in addition to my work as an Industry Analyst *and* Account Manager.

It was an exhausting load, but my Industry Director began to notice my efforts, and the other team members made my work well-known to her as well. After a few months, she shared with me how impressed she was that I had just stepped in without being asked and how much the team had appreciated my leadership. But the most gratifying part was when she admitted she had not known my managerial capabilities before, but now she did.

It was too late for me to become the Pod Manager of the California Auto Team. We had hired the strong Account

Executive and I knew she would serve the team well. But when one door closes, another one opens. The Automotive Industry Director soon approached me about a new opening reporting directly to her as a hybrid Senior Account Executive, a new role across multiple sales channels. It was not a management role, but it would at least give me a chance to get out of analysis and spend more time with clients and a team. I loved working with this particular Industry Director and was simply ready to try something new. I interviewed for the role and was thrilled to earn the position.

I flourished in the job. It came naturally to me and I enjoyed it. Nevertheless, I still felt too comfortable and longed for the challenge of directly managing my own team. I had been serving in the role for about a year when my boss let me know that I was being assigned to a new Pod Manager role. I did not even have to interview for the job, I was being assigned! I had finally reached my major career goal after five years!

It took me longer than I expected to achieve my career objective, but it was worth the wait. Rather than tell people what I could do, I decided to show them. Throughout the process I built a stronger network of peers and leaders who trusted my leadership abilities. They had faith in my decisions and guidance, which made executing ideas much easier. Take the time to prove yourself beyond your current role, and show everyone you are capable of filling the position you want to have. You will earn a stronger support group and confidence along the way.

BUILD DEEP RELATIONSHIPS

Any sales and marketing class will address the importance of building relationships in business. However, I learned at Google that working as hard as you can to help a client or business partner achieve their goals is not enough to build a strong relationship. You have to take the time to truly understand who he or she is as a *person*, to understand his or her situation and motives, and then prove you are genuinely concerned about his or her priorities. Only then can you start to build the foundation for a profound partnership.

When I was volunteering as an Account Manager in addition to my full-time role as an Industry Analyst, I was assigned the most important account for the Southern California Automotive team. I knew all eyes were on me from both the client's side and Google, and there was no room for error. I was well-aware that the client would be demanding of me, but I also understood that the client was under extreme pressure itself as a public company. There were goals that needed to be met and it was my job to help achieve them.

Google's Southern California Automotive Pod hired a new Account Executive just as I took on my voluntary role. Ironically, the new Account Executive had formerly worked for the advertising agency supporting my client. He had played a critical role on that team and was yet to be replaced. As a result, the agency was understaffed and facing tremendous stress to get everything accomplished.

My first week on the job, a member of the agency team emailed me to ask for help in an area of business that Googlers were forbidden to support. I explained that I was unable to assist her according to company policy and guided her to an online help center. I did not receive any response after some time and assumed all was well. On the contrary, little did I know that drama was about to erupt like a volcano.

59

While I presumed all was calm, the agency team member began a rampage and contacted other key people at Google she had previously worked with to express her fury with her new Account Manager (me). I started to receive phone calls and emails from other Googlers she had contacted. She never reached out to me directly. I was embarrassed and felt my face burn red. I had barely even begun working as an Account Manager and already my colleagues were going to think I could not control my clients!

I decided immediately to tackle the problem head on and called the agency team member directly. When she answered the phone, she went straight into a tirade about how unhelpful I was and ended the conversation by hanging up the phone. I did not get a chance to even speak one sentence during the conversation.

My heart was pounding but I knew I had done the right thing. There were good reasons supporting this company policy, and it was in everyone's best interest, including the client's, that the policy was followed. But I still wanted to have a good relationship with my client. I did not want to start with such harsh feelings against me.

We already had a meeting scheduled for about two weeks later. I decided to go to the meeting and act as if nothing had happened. No hard feelings. I would not bring up the conversation and hoped we could just move forward. But I wanted to be prepared in case the agency team member came ready to battle. I needed to understand her better so I could relate to her and show her I really wanted to help.

I sought out our new Account Executive as he had spent quite a bit of time working with this woman. I asked if he could share any insights with me regarding her working style. Perhaps if I could adjust my style in a way that better suited her, we could have a decent relationship. I learned that this woman was severely overloaded on both a professional and personal level, yet she was passionate about her work and wanted to excel.

I came to the conclusion that this woman just had a lot of frustration building up inside and I happened to cross her path at terribly bad time. I became a scapegoat. This might make some people mad, but this perspective was a relief that made me relax. Her reaction was not personal nor was it my fault. As a leader, though, it was my responsibility to help us both get past this unpleasant episode and build a strong relationship.

I went into the meeting and made it a point to speak with this particular agency team member before the meeting began. I asked about her work, her family, her hobbies, but never once mentioned the outrage. In return, she was polite but formal, and we were able to proceed with the meeting smoothly.

At the end of the meeting, she asked to speak with me privately outside of the conference room. I braced myself for a stern lecture and tried to calm the nervous knots forming in my stomach. But my fear was unnecessary. She had pulled me aside to apologize.

I could see this was a woman who was simply overworked. She had good intentions. She was not a mean person. She was just burned out. I learned that in addition to her extra heavy workload at the agency, she was also a single mom who cared deeply for her daughter. This woman just needed a break.

I stopped her before she could finish her apology and told her it was unnecessary. I understood. And she knew that I really did understand. We shared a hug and I left the meeting feeling like I was floating on air. We were going to have a fantastic relationship after all despite our initial turmoil.

We ended up working so well together that even after my time as an Account Manager ended, this woman sought me out at industry conferences to say hello. I genuinely enjoyed working with her, and appreciated the lesson she taught me. If I had not taken the time to understand who she really was as a person and the situation she was going through, I might have taken personal offense to her actions. It would have been hard to pretend like nothing happened if I did not recognize the pressure she was facing. This woman was not furious with me because I followed company policy. She was frustrated because she was overworked, understaffed, and just needed some help. I recognized that she needed assistance, and once she understood I truly wanted to help her as well, we made a great team.

Everyone has a bad day. Everyone makes mistakes. If you can figure out the true meaning behind an issue, you can work together to move forward. I took the time to thoroughly know who she was as a person, and that is what allowed us to build a strong relationship. Take the time to deeply understand who you are working with as *people*. Then you can really build strong, ever-lasting relationships and achieve goals together.

JUST SAY NO

Time is absolutely the most valuable resource, but it took me awhile to really understand that. I have always had a tendency to sacrifice my own time just to make others happy. However, after I was married, I began to view my time as a resource instead of a commodity. I realized that it was in fact within my power to control my hectic schedule into something manageable, but first I had to be comfortable saying no.

Googlers are fascinating people, and the company offered a collaborative environment that made it easy to be friends with your co-workers. It also made it extremely difficult to tell them no. There were many times that I was called upon with little or no notice to fly across the country and help out at a last-minute client meeting or presentation. For years I never said no, even during the times when my peers procrastinated and forced me into a scrambling situation. I was willing to do whatever it took to help my team and drive the business forward.

However, this was not helping others in the long-term. I was teaching them that it was okay to slack in advanced preparation, that I would always be willing to pinch hit. Someone even called me during my honeymoon to ask me to travel to a client meeting on my first day back in the office!

I did in fact travel to that meeting, but suddenly I began to despise traveling so much and on short notice. The way I managed my time no longer impacted just me, but it impacted my husband as well. It was time for me to make a change.

A few months later during the fall of 2011, a large conference was scheduled in Las Vegas and many of Google's Automotive clients were attending. This conference was an annual event hosted by an automotive organization, and I had given a presentation there the previous year just as a favor to help out another Googler. I was planning on attending the conference during the fall of 2011 to meet a few of my clients. I had scheduled my meetings with them far in advance so I could maximize efficiency and minimize the length of my stay. I also led an online seminar for the conference to help out other Googlers, even though none of my own clients would benefit from the seminar due to its topics.

Thus, I was surprised when the same manager who called me during my honeymoon approached me to speak at a conference session on her behalf. The event she was supposed to speak at was scheduled on a Monday morning which happened to be Halloween. She would have had to fly out Sunday night to make it in time, and miss Halloween with her kids. She was quite blunt that she did not want to miss Halloween with her children. I completely respected that and empathized with her. But I had already done more than my share to help Google with this conference, and none of my clients were attending this session. There were others who could help her, including people who directly reported to her. I did not directly report to her, but worked very closely with her on a pilot program and thus treated her with the respect a senior leader deserved.

I tried to help her find an alternative solution. I suggested a manager who directly reported to her and had clients attending that session whom I thought would be better suited for the task. She immediately dismissed the idea because the person I suggested was traveling the week before for business and also had kids. This response infuriated me, because I was traveling all the time to support the business, not just a week before the conference. Furthermore, I felt that my time was not being viewed as equally valuable simply because I did not yet have children. Suddenly, I was adamant about not speaking at this conference which would extend my trip by two days and cut into my weekend.

I conferred with my boss before taking a hard stance against the speaking engagement and she agreed. It was not my place to fill in for this manager. And with my supervisor's support, I declared that I was not available to speak. I also offered several names of people who I thought would be excellent possible speakers and benefit from the experience as well. The manager who asked me to speak was furious. But I had to say no. Everyone's time is valuable, regardless of their personal situation. It was time for me to treat my own time as valuable and respect myself.

She did finally find a replacement other than me, and someone who had clients attending the session. Unfortunately, there was a change in my relationship with this manager after I declined to fill in for her. Though it saddened me, this decline was inevitable. There were numerous other times I had helped out simply to do a favor and yet because I said no once she developed a grudge against me. I really cared for this manager as a person, so it was a bit hurtful, but my time deserved to be respected, too. It was better for the business to have the right person speak at the event, someone who could engage with their own clients. Not someone who would do well speaking and then waste two days of work and expenses before meeting with her own clients.

It was difficult to say no that first time, especially to someone whom I considered a friend and admired. However, you are ultimately responsible for your own time and schedule. You have to take actions to treat your time as the valuable resource it is. Do not be afraid to say no at the right time. It is not only better for you, but it also improves the efficiency of a business.

BE HONEST

Nothing crushes team morale more than dishonesty. It is impossible to have confidence in your teammates if they are not always 100% honest with you. I never expected to encounter a dishonest colleague at a place like Google, where everyone was so highly educated and motivated. But it did happen, and it demonstrated to me how easily a loss of trust can destroy a team.

When I began working as a Senior Account Executive, my team was young and fresh out of college. There was one other Account Executive on the team who had quite a bit of experience but she was transitioning to another role within the company. My young teammates were used to being the smartest in their class at school and were accustomed to a great deal of praise. They were struggling to admit when they needed help and were easily offended when assistance was offered.

The team had been working together for a few months before I joined them. I could instantly sense their apprehension at my arrival. They viewed me as a challenge rather than a senior peer who could help them grow. Thus, I spent a lot of time observing their ways and listening to them before implementing any changes in our team and business processes. I wanted to earn their trust instead of forcing things upon them. It was frustrating for me to make such slow progress, but I felt the young team deserved extra patience.

However, when a team member lied, I had no choice but to swiftly change course. She had been repeatedly coming into the office late and leaving early, claiming she was ill. Then she would send late night emails around 2am, and come in to work late again the following morning. She whined that she could not possibly arrive on time as she was working too hard and too late into the evening to make up for being ill. Her erratic working hours made it difficult to accomplish things as a team and limited the amount of time everyone was physically together. As a result, the team felt stifled.

Her habits continued for quite some time despite our honest discussions of the problems she was causing. Finally, I could no longer tolerate the direction the team was headed and addressed the issue with her direct manager. We agreed that she needed to start coming to work earlier along with her peers, and her direct manager promised to enforce punctuality.

The team decided to give our tardy partner another chance for a fresh start. Yet we soon received a disturbing email from her just a few hours before an important client meeting. Her message announced that she was ill and unable to join the meeting. Our schedule was booked solid all morning, which meant someone had to scramble to master her portion of the presentation. I was the most senior member of the team so I volunteered before anyone could panic. Though we were skeptical of the illness and flustered by the additional workload, we still decided to give her the benefit of the doubt.

But when people lie, the truth eventually comes out. That evening, our Account Executive was surprised by her husband with tickets to a local concert. And who did she happen to see at that concert...none other than our ill teammate, along with her boyfriend who was visiting from out of town. Needless to say, my team was *furious!* All along we had all been covering for someone whom we thought was ill, when in fact she was out having fun! It was absolutely scandalous.

I asked our Account Executive to speak with the direct manager, as she was the one who witnessed our teammate at the concert, not me. The direct manager handled the situation, but our tardy teammate missed yet another opportunity to reconcile her behavior. She never admitted her mistake or apologized to us. In fact, she completely ignored it.

That killed the tiny bit of team chemistry we had left. If she had taken the time to genuinely apologize to our team, to admit her mistakes to us, we could have moved forward. Unfortunately, she chose to feign innocence and did not respect the team. She soon made it well-known that she wanted to transition to a different area of business at Google, and we did everything possible to expedite her move. We had no problem taking on extra work to cover her absence as she transitioned teams. We were already covering for her anyway, but now at least we were in control of our situation. Team morale improved tremendously when she left despite the strenuous workload.

It is far better to be short-handed on a team than to deal with a dishonest teammate. I will take on double the workload before I will compensate for a lying colleague. There is no team without trust, only fear and problems. Today's workload is already demanding without the complications caused by lying. Accept nothing but honesty from your teammates because you cannot build a team with lies.

EARN YOUR RESPECT

Though I never enjoyed working for an automaker, I am grateful for the experience as it gave me an opportunity to know what it was like to feel unappreciated at work. I always felt like a number, almost even a robot, as opposed to a person, despite the fact that I was consistently a top performer in my region. As a result, I made extra efforts for my own team at Google to feel valued. But respect is a privilege, not an entitlement, and I discovered that some young employees struggled to understand that respect must be earned.

As a Senior Account Executive, I was leading a very young team that had a misguided vision of the corporate world. They had never worked full-time in any other professional environment and assumed Google's perks were the minimum standard. Oftentimes I would overhear complaints about silly things like the poor selection of bagels the company had provided for breakfast and I could not help but laugh. I imagined how they never would have survived one week at the automaker, where we did not even leave our own snacks in the office because we were afraid of mice in the building.

Nevertheless, I knew first-hand that a team needs to feel like its leaders believed in them, that they are valuable contributors. Thus, I went the extra mile to do just that. My team was based in Michigan, while I was based in California to be closer to clients. I would travel every quarter to Michigan just to spend time in person with them, even though it meant significantly more work for me. I highlighted their great accomplishments on a weekly basis in team meetings, and praised their efforts to senior management whenever possible. I wanted my team to know that I believed in them and that I noticed and honored their hard work.

However, I also believe in holding people accountable for their actions, and when one team member was not performing up to par, I was not afraid to tell her. I needed to be honest with her about her performance. It was in her best interest to know the reality of her work. I regularly offered her constructive criticism and highlighted things she had done well. Sadly, her efforts simply were not enough and she was struggling to change.

I had made several attempts to put her in the team spotlight in a positive way, but she had managed to destroy every opportunity. Instead of accepting the praise, she would be upset because she was not portrayed as the team super star. She wanted to be lauded for *everything*, yet failed to acknowledge the significant room for improvement. I had worked with her to create a developmental plan for her performance, but unfortunately she consistently produced only excuses instead of results at each check-in. Finally, during a regular one-on-one meeting with her, I had to express disappointment at the lack of progress. I asked what she felt was holding her back to see if there was perhaps something else I could do to help. In return, she said, "I'm a millennial. I need to feel appreciated."

I was floored. In fact, I think my eyes may have popped out of my head a bit. I had done everything possible to make my teammate feel appreciated. If anything, I had erred on the side of too much positive reinforcement. Her response was so disappointing; I did not want to believe she had uttered those words. I wanted it to be a bad joke.

Unfortunately, she was quite serious. And so it was time for me to take a drastically different approach, and be explicitly clear. I explained to her that respect is a privilege, not an entitlement, and it is earned by producing results. While I appreciated her as a person and as a member of our team, she was not pulling her weight and that absolutely was not appreciated. I cited specific examples where I had tried to put her in a positive public spotlight, along with numerous instances of her performance missing objectives. She did not receive the feedback well, and I felt troubled. She refused to recognize any failures on her part. I had no choice left but to turn over her performance issues to her direct supervisor, who further struggled to make progress. Soon after, our problematic teammate left the company to work in a completely unrelated industry.

Though I lamented my unsuccessful attempts to guide our troubled co-worker, my disappointment was soon reversed when I noticed that my remaining teammates had an increased amount of respect for me. She had made them aware of our conversations in an attempt to pit them against me. Rather than pity her, they were proud that they worked with someone honest like me who would hold everyone equally accountable. They were relieved that I was not afraid to take a stand.

We all make mistakes and have opportunities to grow, but what separates a leader from the rest is the ability to acknowledge weaknesses and strive for improvement. Refusing to accept constructive feedback and change is detrimental. You cannot have a solid team without respect. By showing your team that respect has to be earned (and by holding yourself to the same standard), you will all become stronger.

MAKE IT COUNT

Google offered employees a tremendous amount of opportunity to challenge themselves and push their thinking to higher levels than ever before. However, in order to successfully execute creative programs and projects, a great deal of tedious, mind-numbing work was required, too. It could be quite boring and mentally draining, but it was absolutely necessary to succeed. I found younger employees felt especially frustrated in these situations, but I strove to teach my team that every assignment, no matter how small or boring, is in fact a huge opportunity to prove yourself and you need to make it count.

I had to do my fair share of grunt work throughout my career at Google, but it was easier for me to tolerate as I could see the bigger picture. I knew I was demonstrating my dedicated work ethic and that the more challenging opportunities would come. I had an understanding of how critical the tedious tasks were to the success of the company. I tried to explain this to some of the younger employees I mentored who were struggling to find importance and feel a sense of self-worth in their work. I could sense their skepticism, though, and knew I needed another way to convince them.

And then I remembered someone I had mentored earlier in my career, who had begun working for Google as an Administrative Assistant. She had a degree from a Big 10 university and was well-traveled. She was not a naive college graduate, but rather savvy and had a strong sense of purpose. She had a deep desire to work for Google but for reasons unknown to me she was not able to obtain an entry-level position. Perhaps there were no openings at the time she graduated college, perhaps the competition was too fierce, but regardless of the reason, she refused to give up. Instead, she applied for a position as an Administrative Assistant for Industry Directors and was accepted.

While she worked as an Administrative Assistant, she took on any additional projects she could to help her Industry Directors' teams. I had the privilege of mentoring her and teaching her about the automotive industry and was inspired by her positive attitude and strong work ethic. She never once complained about her administrative duties. On the contrary, she was grateful that she had been given an opportunity to become a Googler and prove herself.

She was loved by many due to her positive energy and determination, and it was only a matter of time before she transitioned into a role on the sales team that was more appropriate for her skill level. Furthermore, there were several other Administrative Assistants throughout the company who followed similar paths. They were highly educated and skilled, but for whatever reason were not able to obtain a position on a sales team immediately. Nevertheless, they did not give up. They seized the opportunities available to them and they made it count. They worked with dignity and pride and motivated those around them.

Thus, I was able to share these stories with my younger team and prove to them that no matter how boring a task may be, you have to make it count. Take advantage of every single opportunity to prove your character, your work ethic, and demonstrate a positive attitude that will inspire others. No task is beneath you, and no assignment is too insignificant to prove yourself. Make it count, and you will be surprised how the smallest assignment can in fact make a huge difference and help establish your reputation.

BELIEVE IN A COMMON GOAL

When I worked for an automaker, I was once tasked with leading a cross-functional team to determine which safety features would be included in an upcoming vehicle launch. It was a strenuous assignment, because everyone had a different personal goal. The finance team focused on profit, the engineers focused on safety, the marketing team focused on consumer research, and all were at odds with each other about what really should be included. But at Google, everyone from engineering to sales to temporary staff was focused on one thing only: the end user. Having a common goal that everyone believed in made it much easier to tackle challenging situations.

Google was constantly testing new products in an effort to improve the user experience. The sales teams served as the front line collecting feedback from clients. Sometimes clients loved features, and sometimes they did not. They understood Google's continuous testing. My team faced one situation, though, where a client was not at all pleased with a testing change, and I had to bear the heat.

Google had eliminated a testing feature in Search that the client had found particularly useful. The client could not understand why Google would want to eliminate something that was so helpful to them. I explained that while it may have been helpful to them at the time, the overall goal is to create a better user experience, and that would help my client even more in the long run. My client did not want to hear it and insisted I reach out to the product team that had conducted the test.

I did reach out to the product team, and an engineer was extremely gracious with his time to help me. The test had not proved to create a better user experience, and thus the feature in question was eliminated. There were no plans to bring back this feature. This particular engineer was even so kind as to offer to speak with my client to demonstrate that his sales representative (me) had shared the concern, but we had to act in the best interest of the user.

My client was unfortunately not appeased by access to the product team and instead threatened to cease spending on advertising with Google until the feature was returned. This was a major client of mine, and I could not make my quota without their spending.

I told them I understood their frustration, but we had to look at the big picture of what was best for the user. I again explained that in the long run, working to maximize the user experience would benefit everyone the most, including the client. If we could not help create a great experience for Search users, we would be harming the client more than helping them.

Despite my genuine efforts, the client did in fact cut back their spending and I missed my quota. But it did not matter, because I was part of something bigger than a quota. I was part of a company where everyone truly believed in a common goal, which was to focus on the user. And that filled me with a great deal of pride, more than hitting a quarterly quota ever could.

Without a common goal, you are leaving your employees subject to unnecessary stress in difficult situations. On the contrary, a goal that unites an organization makes it easy for people to decide how to act during challenging times. It is the best way to prepare for the unexpected. Having a common goal that everyone in your organization believes in will provide focus and strength for all stakeholders and help people follow the right course regardless of personal consequences.

ADMIT WHAT YOU DO NOT KNOW

One of my favorite aspects of working at Google was speaking at educational public presentations. I loved the preparation involved and the adrenaline rush from a big audience. Despite my meticulous preparations, there were times I faced questions and did not have the answers. And in those situations, I learned it was best to admit I did not know the solution.

I wanted to perfect my public speaking abilities at Google, and the company encouraged learning by offering classes. I took all the local classes I could and once I even traveled to San Francisco for a few days to attend a course focused on public speaking. The classes gave me more structure for my preparation routine and more confidence to speak before bigger audiences.

Whenever I was scheduled for a public speaking opportunity, I spent days preparing. I aimed to be a subject matter expert. I studied current news related to the topic at hand and anticipated possible questions. I researched the latest press regarding Google. I wanted to know what people outside the company were thinking and which Google products were creating a buzz amongst consumers. I devoted so much time and energy to preparing and delivering a presentation that I was completely exhausted once it was over. But I always felt a great deal of satisfaction in educating others, which made all the work worthwhile.

Thus, I was honored when a client invited me to speak at a private conference he had scheduled for his company. His company had blocked out an entire day for senior members and executives to be educated about critical business topics, and digital media happened to be one of them. I traveled from my home base in California to their headquarters in Florida and felt privileged to be a part of their educational day.

I worked with a teammate to design an educational and entertaining presentation. The day of the conference, I sailed through my portion of the presentation and reached the question and answer period. I had smoothly addressed all of the questions and had just a minute or two left before my time on stage was up. Then an audience member inquired about a new Google experiment that I had never heard of. I had spent quite a bit of time researching Google's latest experiments anticipating such questions, but this one I knew absolutely nothing about.

I stayed strong and did not hesitate. I directly answered the gentleman by saying that is not something I am familiar with, but I will be happy to look into it and get back to you. And then I moved on to the next question.

Afterward, I was approached by my client who had invited me to speak. I always enjoyed working with him because he was so direct and honest about what he needed for his business. His openness enabled us to be true partners as opposed to having a vendor/consumer relationship. I valued his opinion tremendously and was anxious for his feedback. I was humbled by his remarks, as he began by sharing how much he respected me for admitting I did not know the answer to the gentleman's question. He went on to praise my work and claimed he knew I would be going places.

I was shocked by how much of an impact my honesty had made. It has never occurred to me to lie or make up an answer to something I do not know. I was surprised and honored to be able to build trust and a stronger relationship with my client simply by being myself. (I did of course follow up and confirm the correct answer after the presentation, though.)

No one has the solution to every question, and no one expects you to have the answer to every inquiry immediately. But people do expect you to tell them when you do not know the answer. You will not impress anyone by making something up. Instead, you will make yourself look like a fool. Admit what you do not know, and then be sure to follow up and figure it out. Everyone will respect your honesty and admire your work ethic when you later follow through with the appropriate response.

REMEMBER YOUR STARS

One of the things that separate Google from other companies is that it is a place where your peers are expected to help you to the best of their abilities. It is an understood part of the company's culture. It makes for an incredibly collaborative environment, but it also adds a great deal of pressure to a team when there is a low performer. It is assumed that everyone will contribute to help the low performer improve and succeed, which ideally should benefit the overall efforts of the team. Unfortunately, it is easy to neglect your star performers in these situations and that in fact is detrimental to a team.

During my time as a Senior Account Executive, I was challenged with an extremely low performing teammate. She was not only considered a poor contributor on the team, but also the lowest performer in entire Automotive Vertical. My team was part of a pilot program and our success was crucial to the success of the Automotive Vertical. In addition, my small team was understaffed and having a sub-par performer placed a terrible burden upon us.

To further exacerbate the situation, our low performer had an attitude problem. She was not receptive to feedback, and this made it increasingly frustrating for the team to guide her. My other two teammates had reached a point where they no longer felt comfortable sharing constructive criticism and spent most of their time with her in silence. Thus, I found myself spending the majority of my time attempting to mentor her and help her improve. It was the Google way to do everything possible to bring a teammate up to par.

I hoped that by spending more time with our low performer, we would see improvement not only in her performance, but also in team morale. My remaining teammates were feeling shattered between their heavy workloads and the stress of working with such a negative person. It was her attitude more than her poor work that drained our team. I thought that I could relieve pressure for them by taking on the heavy load of mentoring her. I had no choice but to trust that my other two performers could guide themselves. I had a lot of faith in them because they were positive people who cared about doing the right thing for clients. Their determination made them the stars of the team in my eyes.

While I spent most of my time working with our low performer, I continued regular check-ins with my stars. I noticed, though, that their positive energy had not reemerged despite my extra efforts. I asked one of them to be honest with me about how they were feeling. And a shocking truth came out. He had begun to question his own performance and view himself as a poor performer because I was spending so little time with him.

I felt as if someone had punched me in the stomach when I heard this. How could I have let my stars feel so low? I still feel nauseous to this day when I recall that conversation. I cared about these people as if they were my own little family, and I had let them down. I gathered my stars together for a direct discussion. They had a chance to express their feelings, and I made it clear to them how much I respected them and their work. I apologized for not recognizing their frustration sooner, but also encouraged them to come forward with their concerns in the future. They could not be afraid to voice their issues with me, no matter how busy I appeared, as that only created more problems.

After that conversation, my stars were revived. They knew they were in good standing with me, and they had regained confidence in their work. I made extra effort to check in with them more frequently, too. Our low performer soon ended up leaving the company for an opportunity that was a better fit for her.

My team's morale soared even further once our low performer was no longer an issue, despite carrying an even heavier workload. It is amazing how productive positive energy can be. My team taught me that no matter what is happening at the office, you cannot neglect your stars. They still need attention and encouragement, especially when they are young. Spending more time with my stars was good for me, too, as I was motivated by their positive energy. Do not take for granted people's outstanding efforts. Make sure they know you recognize their results and are always willing to hear their concerns, no matter how busy you may be.

CARE FOR YOUR PEOPLE

Actions always speak louder than words, and I was truly touched by the lengths some managers went through at Google to show their teams they cared about them. I was fortunate enough to have such managers myself, and they inspired me to always go the extra mile for the company and later my own team. I had never been treated with such kindness when I worked for the automaker, and I realized what a difference it makes in a corporate culture when you really care for your people.

I was traveling extensively when I was a Senior Account Executive in 2010, and I was also planning my wedding reception. My husband was living overseas at the time, and we had lived a world apart from each other the entire duration of our relationship. We agreed that we would not continue a long-distance relationship after our wedding reception, but we both had professional obligations that needed to be met. He was bound by a contract to serve a specific period of time with his company. Meanwhile, I was limited by my vacation days and could only be gone from work for so long.

My nerves tingled as I debated my situation, and I wondered if it was possible to take a short unpaid leave of absence from Google. I scheduled time to speak with my boss and ask her opinion. I did not want to jeopardize my career and have people think poorly of me for taking a leave of absence. However, I had reached a point where I owed it to myself to make an extra effort for my personal life. I needed to know my options.

I explained my dilemma to my supervisor and awaited her response. I wanted to know if it was possible to take such a leave of absence, and if so what were the real consequences. *How would I be perceived by senior leadership? Would I still be on track for promotion? Would I ruin my strong reputation?* These are a few of the questions that silently raced through my mind. I fidgeted anxiously as she began to speak. But her words surprised me. She was discussing possible projects I could work on overseas. She was calculating how much time I could spend working on such projects and any assignment she could possibly create and present to Human Resources so that I could maintain my strong contributions and not have to take an unpaid leave.

I was floored. This woman cared about me so much, she was afraid to let me go on an unpaid leave. She thought I was coming to her for help to spend more time with my husband without losing pay. I was so astonished I could not even explain that I was inquiring about an *unpaid* leave. I could feel her genuine concern in my heart and it made me beyond grateful to be working for someone who cared about me so much. I was stunned into silence.

Fortunately, things worked out and my husband was able to relocate with me immediately after our wedding reception. But to this day, I will do anything I can to help this former manager of mine, and several others I crossed paths with at Google, because they demonstrated a sincere consideration for me as person. They truly cared about my well-being, and that kind of attention is a powerful motivator. I kept these lessons close to my heart as a team manager, and tried to compensate for various personal situations as much as possible to keep my employees happy while still being fair. Show your people that you really care for them, and you will be rewarded with a highly motivated, happy, and loyal team forever.

PREPARE TO SUCCEED

Shortly after I became a manager at Google, all sales employees were asked to add a few words that described their personal motto to their internal online profile. This came easily to me, as my motto has always been "prepare to succeed." Sometimes it felt like business moved faster than the speed of light at Google, but because I consistently dedicated time with my team to prepare for as much as we could possibly anticipate, we always found some room to breathe. Our preparation enabled us to do more than just survive and succeed. It allowed us to flourish.

Our objectives were measured in quarters, and 90 days flew by faster than you could imagine. We did not have the luxury of waiting until the beginning of the quarter to set our plan of action. Thirty days before the end of the current quarter, I gathered my team together to plan for the following quarter. I wanted them to feel as if our plan was really *our* plan, that they had significant input into our goals and strategy. Thus, we would begin by hosting a brainstorming session. Everyone was expected to share ideas, and in this initial meeting no idea was eliminated. It was okay to ask questions to better understand an idea, but no critical questions were allowed. It created a safe space where people were not afraid to speak their minds.

After our initial brainstorming session, we would reconvene to prioritize our list. We grouped our objectives by the number of days needed to accomplish: 30, 60, or 90 days. I called this our 30-60-90 plan. Prioritizing helped give the team focus, and then it was more about what we needed to do as opposed to who had the best ideas. My team was young, and they could easily be offended if they thought others simply did not like their ideas. I needed them to stay focused on objective facts, and prioritizing eliminated skepticism. It also helped the team seriously consider what they could realistically accomplish in a quarter.

Next, we began to reach out to clients. I knew that our clients

84

were just as busy as we were, and they always appreciated advanced planning. Each quarter, we were able to secure in-person meetings with key contacts at all of our clients because we planned ahead. Too many times I saw other teams struggle to get a meeting because they did not anticipate how much notice a client would need to fit them in. I did not want our clients to "pencil us in," I wanted to be a regular partner that they *needed* to meet with. As a result of our preparation, we were able to regularly meet with clients and create value for them.

The plan was especially helpful to promote our work internally to senior management. I always shared our plan with our Industry Director before the quarter began, and regularly provided updates throughout the quarter how we were performing against our objectives. Despite all of our meticulous planning, there were times when we did not meet all of our goals. Nevertheless, we could look back on our 30-60-90 plan and see what actions worked and where we fell short, and make adjustments for the following quarter. Furthermore, I explained to my team that if we did meet every objective, then we failed to set the right targets. I wanted to challenge ourselves and always strive for the best possible. It was okay if we missed sometimes so long as we were trying. As the saying goes, reach for the moon and if you fall, at least you will land amongst the stars.

Sometimes it was difficult to rally my team to take time away from an existing quarter to plan for the next, especially when we were not meeting our current objectives. But as a leader, it was my responsibility to help them find motivation. In these cases, I tried to make our brainstorming sessions a little more fun with things like pizza and favorite snacks, attention to little details that would make my team remember how much I cared about them. There was one instance when I was visiting team members in Michigan and they were incredibly frustrated with our progress. I spontaneously made them stop everything and leave the office to get Slurpees from a nearby 7-11. Our Slurpee run took a total of about 30 minutes, but they were completely different people when we returned to the office and their new positive energy was reflected in their ideas and work.

It is not always easy to find time to prepare for the future when you are struggling in the present, but it is absolutely necessary. It is impossible to succeed consistently without preparation. Making time to prepare for the future helps your team feel focused and it gives them more opportunities to feel like ownership of the strategy as well. It helps sets expectations for everyone and even makes it easier to evaluate performance afterward. No matter how busy you may be, you must find time to prepare for the future, and as a result you will be amazed by how much more your team can achieve.

THINK BEYOND YOURSELF

It is easy to become laser-focused on your own workload when you are in a demanding job. However, it is even more important in such an environment to think about how you can help your boss with his or her role, beyond just doing your own job well. Those who are able to anticipate the needs of their leaders quickly stand out from their peers. At Google I often thought about what my supervisor needed and how I could make his or her life easier. My intentions were purely to assist others, but I was pleasantly surprised by how these actions helped me, too.

I spent a lot of time observing people at Google, both managers and non-managers. I noticed that non-managers were too demanding of their bosses. Non-managers expected their bosses to clear all hurdles for them so they could focus exclusively on clients. That is typical of a sales organization. But Google's managers were expected to play a heavy role in sales, too. Some of them were on the road meeting with clients every single week. And like most organizations, managers were heavily bogged down with unavoidable internal reports and meetings.

My first boss at Google is the one who inspired me to pay so much attention to the demands on her time, because I truly wanted to help her. She led with enthusiasm and energy despite her hectic schedule, and never let her sales team feel her pressure. I genuinely wanted to relieve her because she was doing so much to assist everyone else. I tried to anticipate her needs for internal and external meetings, and arm her with the right information before she could even ask for it. Soon it became part of my regular routine and I did not even consider it as extra work, but as the job I needed to do.

I continued to work like this for all of my bosses at Google, but as I grew with the company I was able to think more like a manager and help my supervisors even more. I especially looked for ways to save them time as that was everyone's most valuable (and limited) resource. Simple things like creating templates for the entire team to submit information could spare them hours of precious time. Every time I communicated information to a boss, I made sure it was as efficiently as possible.

Then one day when I was a manager myself, my boss surprised me in a team meeting. She had recently asked all of the managers who reported directly to her to submit a summary of their quarterly accomplishments. I had taken great pains to ensure my summary was as clear and concise as it could be. But as it contained my personal accomplishments, I considered it a private document and did not share it. Consequently, I felt my face burn bright red during our team meeting when I unexpectedly saw my report projected on a screen for all my peers to see. My supervisor had shared it and asked that everyone submit their report in the same format moving forward.

This was one template that I had not distributed amongst my peers as it was all about my own achievements, and that felt a little bit too much like bragging for me. I was quite embarrassed that it was now an example for all, though I was glad it had been so helpful for my boss. Yet my surprise continued when a fellow manager called me in distress after the meeting. He was frustrated because his summary had looked nothing like mine, and he was afraid that he had missed our boss's initial request to present information that way. I could sense his confusion and I knew he feared that he did not have a strong relationship with our boss.

I put his mind at ease and explained the situation. She never asked any of us, including myself, to submit the information in a particular format. I simply thought about what would be most helpful if I were in her shoes. *How would I want to see the results? How could I easily aggregate and compare? What would help me save time and still have everything I needed to make a decision?* I thought about the situation from her perspective and crafted a solution that I thought would be most efficient.

That conversation with my peer is what made me realize just how important it is to think like a boss. Doing your daily job is not enough to stand out from your peers. You have to go a step further and demonstrate that you know what it is like to be in a leader's position, and how to get things done efficiently. My original goal in thinking like my supervisors was just to help them, but I gained a lot in return, too. I proved myself as a stronger performer and leader who had the team's best interest at heart. Think like your supervisor and see how a different perspective can help you drive efficiency for others and yourself, too.

LET THEM FLY

Growing up in Michigan, I dreamed of having a long, successful career with an American automaker. Unfortunately, when I began working full-time for an automotive company, I felt frustrated and stifled in my work. As a result, I decided to apply to graduate schools much earlier than I originally intended. I have always believed in full transparency, and thus I shared my educational plans with my boss at the time. He immediately laughed in my face, and told me I would never make it. Throughout the application process, he harassed me and tried to persuade me to give up. The truth was he simply did not want to lose me as I was one of the region's top performers. His laughter infuriated me and made my blood boil, but he taught me how important it is for a manager to let his or her team members fly when it is time for them to go.

From the moment I began leading my team of direct reports at Google, we were severely understaffed. Our Account Executive was out on maternity leave. She had never actually worked as an Account Executive before, but she had excelled as an Account Manager and shared with her boss that she was ready for a new challenge. I could have refused to give her a chance on my team and argued that I needed someone immediately due to our tremendous workload. However, I believe in taking a risk on hard-working, honest people. I was willing to offer her an opportunity to grow in a new role on my team, even if it meant being understaffed for several months. I welcomed her onto my team and waited anxiously for her return to work.

When she did resume working, she fit in quite well with my team and demonstrated an eagerness to learn. I was happy to have her on board and to guide her. I made my best efforts to be flexible with her personal schedule as she was a new mom and I wanted her to succeed both at work and at home. I felt relieved to finally have some more help and so did my other employees. She was based in Michigan, and I was based in California, but I

90

was confident we could make the arrangement work with technology and travel.

Alas, my relief did not last long. After a couple of months, I learned from my boss that another Industry Director, someone much more senior than myself, had approached my Account Executive about moving onto one of her teams in the Detroit office. I was initially furious, but with the Industry Director, not our Account Executive. I was hurt that the Industry Director had not spoken to me about the idea before approaching my team member, especially since I knew this Director so well and considered her a friend. I was not upset with my Account Executive, because if I was her, I likely would have kept silent about the proposal, too. Of course she would follow the more senior company leader! Nevertheless, I do not believe in secrets within a team, so I boldly addressed the subject in our next one-on-one meeting.

I explained to my Account Executive that I was aware she had been approached about another opportunity, and I asked her what she thought about it. I immediately sensed from her description that the new role would offer her more personal flexibility than what I could give her, and I understood how important this was to her. I empathized with her. She had to do what was best for her, and I made it clear that I would fully support whatever she decided. Nevertheless, I did ask her to be open with me and share developments throughout her decision making process. I made it clear that I expected to know when she was being approached by others, though I understood her initial silence.

Our meeting was being conducted through a video conference, and even through the screen I could instantly sense her relief. She had been burdened by the secrecy, and she suffered from guilt as she did not want to let down her fellow teammates. I am sure she had also feared how I would react, knowing the lengths I had gone through to give her the opportunity on my team. Yes,

I was disappointed because she was a strong contributor and a good person, but she had to do what was best for her and her family, and I absolutely supported that.

She did in fact end up leaving my team a few months later, but it was on a good note. There were no hard feelings because letting her fly on her own path was the right thing to do. I know first-hand what it feels like when someone tries to stop you from trying a new opportunity that is a better fit for you. I would never act like my manager at the automaker and try to stop someone from reaching his or her dream. I know from other managers that my Account Executive in return spoke highly of me throughout her office and helped strengthen my reputation as leader. It is not always easy, but when one of your team members has to leave, you have to help them fly away. Support your team members when they find an alternative path that makes them happy, and you will demonstrate your integrity and leadership to everyone.

MAKE TIME TO READ

I was thrilled to discover that most Googlers were always reading something fascinating for personal enjoyment despite their incredulous workloads. Googlers loved to learn and grow, and they did not limit their reading to Internet news or gossip. They read books and they were happy to discuss them. As an avid reader myself, I thrived in this environment and encouraged my team to share their favorite stories with each other. As a result, I found that my teammates and I learned more about each other and we added a new level of fun to our jobs, too.

I was fortunate to have a mother that encouraged reading at a young age. Some of my favorite childhood memories include trips to the library. Reading has always been an important part of my life, and that did not stop when I attended the Harvard Business School. I worried, though, if I would be able to read anything that was not related to work once I started at Google.

My fears were never validated, as I quickly discovered Googlers' passion for books. In fact, several managers gifted books to their team members to provide inspiration. When I became a manager myself, it was immediately evident that my young team missed the intellectual classroom conversations they were accustomed to. I wondered how I could bring that feeling back to them while still driving the business and helping them grow. And it soon became quite clear. My team needed time for books.

I asked team members to share what they were reading in our weekly team meeting. I learned so much myself from these conversations! I was happy to discover new books and ideas from my pod. However, I was even more excited to see the spark of enthusiasm in their faces when they shared their knowledge. I could see that they felt more confident in their daily work because they thought they were contributing and it made them feel intelligent. Everyone just wants to feel smart sometimes. I was also able to see some of my team members really grow in their understanding of business concepts and leadership as a result of books they discussed with each other.

I did like to keep these sessions from getting too serious, though. After all, this was intended to be fun! That is why Dr. Seuss's *Oh, the Places You'll Go!* was one of my favorite books that I gave to my members. It was my whimsical way of teaching my pod that I believed in them. Their happy reactions to the gift were priceless. An incredible marketing book I often recommended was *Different: Escaping the Competitive Herd* by Youngme Moon, who was one of my favorite professors at the Harvard Business School.

There are only so many hours in the day, and far too much to do. However, it is truly a must to make time to read, and it is even better if you can share this hobby with your colleagues. My team was significantly stronger and more confident because we had fun learning from each other about books. It is easy to get absorbed in your work, but reading helps provide an outside perspective. Encourage your team to make time to read, and make time for yourself to read as well. You will quickly notice the difference in your team's outlook and conversations and your team will probably feel smarter, too.

ATTITUDE IS EVERYTHING

Since my early days at Google, I spent a lot of time observing managers and leaders within the company. It was easy to see who was loved by their team and who was not. Surprisingly, I noticed that quota achievement and client status had little to do with a manager's happiness. There were some who regularly hit their challenging objectives and still always seemed miserable. I soon learned that it was really all about attitude, and it does in fact start at the top.

Before I became a manager myself, I spent a lot of time thinking about what I wanted my team to be like. I most certainly wanted a driven team that was ready to work hard to achieve results. But I wanted us to have fun, too. I wanted my team members to enjoy spending time together, to feel like our pod was their little family outside of their real family. Perhaps that was a bit too idealistic, but it was my goal.

Thus, I secretly studied other teams to see what worked and what did not. It was amazing how each pod was a strong reflection of its manager's personality. You could easily pick out a negative pod manager without ever meeting him or her just based on a few conversations with a team. At the same time, it was also evident who the positive pod managers were, and their energy spilled over into their teams like a refreshing waterfall. I began to wonder what motivated these positive managers, and how could they possibly maintain so much energy on a regular basis?

I finally worked up the nerve to ask a manager I admired what was her secret. Like most things in life, there is no secret, but consistent hard work. She shared that she has her own struggles. Sometimes she would come into the office after having had a terrible evening and morning at home, but she never let it show. The minute she stepped foot into the office she was full of bright smiles and a cheerful voice. She knew that everyone was watching her, and she had to lead by example. It took effort and it was exhausting to demonstrate so much positivity consistently, but she understood that the end results would be worth it. She had her eyes on bigger objectives, and in order to motivate her team members, she knew she had to drive their energy levels.

This came as a bit of a shock to me. I had assumed that this positive force just came naturally to her, that it was her personality to be so cheery. On the contrary, it was hard work. It would have been much easier for her to come in and be grumpy sometimes and commiserate. Everyone has those days! But she took a more difficult path and for that she was rewarded.

I later attended an internal conference led by this particular manager, and she created a plaque featuring the poem *Attitude* by Charles R. Swindoll that truly summarized how she led her team each day. Her philosophy was that you cannot control what happens to you, but you most certainly can control how you react to a situation. And that is what makes a positive leader, someone who can still push forth with good energy no matter how frustrating or difficult a dilemma may be.

Admittedly, I found this is much harder in practice than it may seem. There are days when you are forced to work with negative people and it is easy to let them bring you down. You cannot. It is absolutely worth the extra effort to maintain your optimistic momentum. Think about how much more fun it is to be surrounded by happy people as opposed to a group who is constantly whining and complaining. Lead by example and create an upbeat environment for everyone around you by remembering that attitude is everything.

UNDERSTAND YOURSELF

Google had many systems in place for peers and managers to provide feedback regarding someone's performance. The annual performance review system required written peer feedback, and Googlers were not afraid to speak their minds. I found this feedback system to be a key aspect of my continuous learning and growth. However, I realized that no matter how much feedback you receive, you can never truly grow without having a strong understanding of yourself.

I have always been my own harshest critic, and I have gone through too many self-evaluation exercises over the years to count. After a while, many of these tests began to lose their luster and really felt like boring required exercises as opposed to insightful assignments. Thus, I was wary as a manager when our Automotive Industry Director asked everyone to participate in another personality assessment exercise.

Surprisingly, the evaluation test was one I had not tried before. I was skeptical as each individual needed to spend about an hour answering questions about themselves before any results were determined, and the outcomes were not immediately available. While I believe everyone always has more to learn, I doubted there was much I would gain from another programmed personality assessment. I wanted to hear more from other *people* about my performance and personality, not from a computer.

Nevertheless, I dedicated the time necessary to properly answer all the questions, and mandated the same of my team. There was a significant time lag before we received any of the results, and when we did get them, each individual received a personalized binder, not just a few comments, detailing the assessment.

I was immediately impressed by the level of detail in the analysis and how accurate the overview of my personality and working style were. Furthermore, the results included pages and pages of comprehensive descriptions, not just a few general summarizing statements. I was suddenly captivated by this profile evaluation and I did not want to stop reading until I had finished absorbing all 32 pages.

Because I spend a great deal of time evaluating myself on a regular basis, the results were not particularly surprising to me. It was reassuring in a way, as I knew I had a good understanding of myself. Like any profile evaluation, this one included strengths and weaknesses, and I was already cognizant of all the items listed. I learned a few new ways to consider how I may be perceived by others at times, so it was in fact a worthwhile exercise, but still not anything extraordinary. My surprise came later, however, during my one-on-one meetings with my team members to discuss their results. That is when I realized how little some of them actually knew themselves.

Of course, one profile evaluation is not enough to tell people everything they need to know about themselves. But what caught my attention was the fear some of my team members demonstrated as they reviewed their profile results. They were incredibly uncomfortable with parts of the assessment. They did not necessarily disagree, but they were a bit stunned to see some of their personal characteristics printed in black and white.

I wanted this to be a positive learning experience for my team, not a nightmare. Consequently, instead of focusing on specifics stated in the assessment, I framed the exercise as just the beginning of our growth together. I asked some team members to think about the areas that surprised them, if they agreed, and what they wanted to change if anything. I used the evaluations as an excuse to push my team deeper into self-reflection. By focusing on the bigger objective of knowing themselves as opposed to specific words in the assessment, I was able to relieve unnecessary pressure on my team.

As I guided my team through their evaluations, I learned more about myself, too. I have always had a strong sense of self-awareness simply because I am ridiculously hard on myself. I finally understood that it is possible to become self-aware without being too critical of yourself. And even more importantly, my team taught me the consequences of a lack of self-awareness. It breeds feelings of insecurity, and insecurity is nothing but detrimental to a team and its performance. Make it a point to regularly think about your actions, your statements, and how people perceive you. Take the time to plan what you want to change. Tell yourself it is not only okay, but necessary to constantly study yourself, to know who you are and who you want to be. A strong sense of self-awareness will inspire confidence and trust, plus it will enable you to motivate others. If you do not understand yourself, then you will never be able to understand your team and their reactions to you. And that is a must for a true leader.

HAVE SOME FUN

Googlers took a lot of pride in their work, and I was no exception. I struggled not to think about work all the time, and I harshly judged my results. Nothing less than outstanding performance was acceptable for me, and I had no problem sacrificing my personal time to reach that outcome. In hindsight though, I now understand that while my dedication to the job was admirable, I made a huge mistake. I did not let myself have enough fun on the job, and that is my biggest regret.

Googlers carry a massive workload, one that is impossible to accomplish during a typical eight-hour workday. As a result, I made it a habit to work through lunch. Unless I was meeting a client for lunch, 99.5% of the time you could find me working at my desk. I thought if I pushed through lunch, I did not need to feel guilty about taking some time in the evening for myself to work out and catch up with family. There were several people who had a similar mindset, including senior managers. It was not uncommon for them to secretly question, *how did others have time for lunch*? In fact, I feared that my work ethic would be under speculation if I ever did decide to start taking lunch breaks.

On the contrary, though, Google made every effort for Googlers to take a real lunch break and enjoy some time together. The company sought to bring healthy and tasty food to all of its offices, and some offices even had their own personal chefs. I noticed that the majority of the engineering teams would actually take a real lunch break on a regular basis. But there were few who dared to do so amongst the sales teams.

Occasionally during a town hall office meeting, we would talk about a need to boost office morale and how we should have lunch together. Afterward, the senior managers would make a few appearances in the cafeteria and pretend that it was a really enjoyable experience. Nevertheless, we could sense their

100

anxiety to get back to their desks for fear of missing an important email or phone call, and their efforts quickly faded.

There were a few times I was able to force myself away from my desk and enjoy lunch in the café. The truth is this break was not just about having lunch away from the desk. It was about getting to know my peers in a different light. My experience has taught me that there is something about sharing a meal that helps people let their guard down and reveal more about themselves than they would otherwise. The few meals I shared with my colleagues were not just about relaxing for a little bit. They were moments of bonding. I learned about my peers on a personal level, their hobbies, their likes and dislikes, their families, their struggles and their joys. I met people in different departments that I later felt more comfortable reaching out to for help on new projects. I grew my network and made more friends.

I gained all of these benefits from a few lunches, and yet I was still afraid to do it on a regular basis. It was a terrible mindset that I had, and I did not realize until after I left the company what a horrible mistake I had made all those years. To this day, the thing I miss the most about Google is the people. By skipping out on lunch, I cheated myself from amazing experiences with phenomenal people.

I doubt I could have had lunch in the café on a daily basis, but if I could go back in time, I would have at least made it happen once a week. And I would have absolutely made more of an effort to emphasize the importance of doing so with my own team. You need to have some fun in your office on a regular basis. Maybe it is not lunch, maybe it is a regular coffee break or stroll outside or snack time. But it is imperative to get away from your desk and feel more relaxed with your colleagues consistently. You will learn more about each other, you will feel more energized, and when you have more fun you will likely be happier on the job, too. Find a way to have some fun on a regular basis with your peers, and do not waste an opportunity to do so.

BE UNCOMFORTABLE

Larry Page, Google's inspiring co-founder and CEO at the time, always encouraged Googlers to "be a little uncomfortable." He wanted Googlers to be challenging themselves in order to truly innovate. He believed that people who were too comfortable would never really be able to drive change. Thus, when I soon felt stagnant as a manager, I began to wonder if my time at Google was coming to an end.

I had dreamed of becoming a team manager at Google. I had spent about five years trying to reach my goal. I had worked so hard to obtain this position and I could not believe it had finally happened!

And yet after just a couple of months, a surprising disappointment set in. My new role was not nearly as challenging as I had expected.

The role had not differed significantly from my work as a hybrid Senior Account Executive. The major difference was that I was required to do more internal work. I had more internal management meetings and formal reports to complete. In addition, my team was once again understaffed, so I was still acting as a Senior Account Executive while simultaneously serving as a team manager. In other words, I was doing more of the work I did not enjoy, and less of the work I found fulfilling. I was once again challenged by the volume of work as opposed to the type of work I was doing.

I thought that maybe I was simply overloaded and needed a break. I was pregnant at the time, and wondered if perhaps maternity leave would give me enough separation from the company to come back energized and ready to go. I had an option to begin my leave a month before our child was due, but I declined. I wanted to make sure everything was as organized as possible for both my team and clients so that high performance standards could be maintained. I did not want any problems to arise because of a lack of preparation on my part.

I had saved all of my vacation days over the past year, which meant I would be able to take a six-month leave to care for our daughter before coming back to work. I was completely planning on returning to the company after my leave, but changes happen so fast and so frequently at Google that I contemplated what my team manager role would look like when I returned. *Would I have the same team? Would I have the same functions? Would completely new and more interesting roles be created?* Twice throughout my career at Google, I had been assigned to new roles that never existed before. Anything was possible.

I spent so much time and energy preparing my team and clients that I did not even have our nursery ready when I went into labor. Our family had to assemble our child's bed while I was in the hospital. I had a difficult delivery and thus my own recovery was longer and more challenging than expected. The first three months were a struggle for me as I had to learn it is okay to depend on others for help sometimes. Because I had spent so much effort preparing my team and clients, and neglecting my own family, I had vowed to myself that I would abstain from work during my leave. I promised myself to only occasionally check email and touch base with my boss. My family deserved to have my full attention during this period. I kept my promise. But when I began to check in, I felt a disappointment. I was expecting a rush of excitement as I got back into a work mindset. Instead, the emails seemed repetitive and the only change I noticed was increased pressure.

I started to think that perhaps my dream job was simply too similar to my previous role as a Senior Account Executive. Maybe I just needed a completely different role to bring back my passion for the job. I wondered what else I could do at Google. However, in this case my type-A personality worked against me. I cannot do anything without giving it 100 percent. What new role could I do that would still allow me to be a strong force in my child's life?

I felt crushed for some time. My dream job turned out to be a disappointment. It was not all I had hoped it would be. But then I realized something else. I was wrong to focus on my "dream job." What had really mattered all this time was my journey to get to that dream.

It had been an incredible journey, one that I was privileged to experience. I learned more about working with people during my time at Google than any degree could ever have taught me. I had been challenged in ways I never expected, and developed a true understanding of what it takes to be a leader. Being a leader is not about being a manager or having people directly report to you. It is about setting an example *every single day*. It is about working hard to do what is right. It is about standing by your people and putting them ahead of you. It is about how you act every day, how you speak in each conversation, how you communicate every message. It is a daily process and *hard work*. It is not about titles or levels. A true leader will shine through no matter what his or her position or assignment is because a true leader *cares about people*.

Once I realized this, I knew that my time at Google had come to an end. I needed to be brave and step out to "be a little uncomfortable" and find my next journey. Otherwise, I would not be able to keep growing. A true leader is never afraid to seek knowledge and continue learning.

Thus, with a heavy heart, I called my boss a few months into my leave and announced my resignation. While I knew I was making the right decision, it was incredibly bittersweet. I loved working for Google. My colleagues had been like my second family for years. We had been through so many milestone events together…everything from breakups to makeups, promotions, reassignments, weddings, birthdays, funerals, and even new babies. My only consolation was that I knew our bond was strong and we would keep in touch with each other.

I will never be able to replicate my time at Google, nor do I want to. It was a lot like attending college. A phenomenal, life changing experience, but at the end you knew it was time to move on. You will forever feel loyal to your alma mater, but you were ready to tackle something else. I am beyond grateful for the experience I had at Google and I am a better person because of it. I simply reached a point where my own personal learning and growth required me to move in a new direction and find a different dream. I was honored to be a Googler, and I will be forever thankful for the journey.

ABOUT THE AUTHOR

Before she chartered her own course as an entrepreneur, Linda El Awar served as a Head of Industry at Google, where she led a sales team and helped advertisers develop digital marketing strategies across platforms to connect with consumers. In her previous role as a Senior Account Executive, Linda helped advertisers grow their business through digital marketing consulting. Prior to that, as Analysis Manager for the Automotive & Entertainment Verticals at Google, Linda developed data insights including query trends, search benchmarks and growth opportunities across both industries.

Before joining Google in 2007, Linda served as a Zone Manager for an automaker's Customer Service Division working directly with automotive dealerships. She has also worked extensively in retail and consulting businesses. Linda has served on the Board of Directors for the Harvard Business School Alumni Association in Orange County.

Linda holds a BBA with Distinction from the University of Michigan Ross School of Business and an MBA with Second Year Honors from Harvard Business School.

To contact Linda, email: linda@elawar.com
Or follow her on Twitter: @linda_elawar

Made in the USA
San Bernardino, CA
25 April 2016